Alfresco for Administrators

A fast-paced administrator's guide to Alfresco from the administration, managing, and high-level design perspectives

Vandana Pal

[PACKT] PUBLISHING

BIRMINGHAM - MUMBAI

Alfresco for Administrators

First published: April 2016

Production reference: 1250416

Published by Packt Publishing Ltd.
Livery Place
35 Livery Street
Birmingham B3 2PB, UK.

ISBN 978-1-78217-503-2

www.packtpub.com

Credits

Author
Vandana Pal

Reviewers
Johnny Gee
Piergiorgio Lucidi
Giuseppe Urso

Commissioning Editor
Dipika Gaokar

Acquisition Editor
Rahul Nair

Content Development Editor
Mayur Pawanikar

Technical Editor
Anushree Arun Tendulkar

Copy Editor
Safis Editing

Project Coordinator
Nidhi Joshi

Proofreader
Safis Editing

Indexer
Rekha Nair

Production Coordinator
Aparna Bhagat

Cover Work
Aparna Bhagat

About the Author

Vandana Pal is a software engineer and author. She currently works as senior consultant at CIGNEX Datamatics.

She has extensive experience working with Enterprise Digital Asset Management and Content Management Systems. She has worked with various deployments of Alfresco in various domains, such as media, finance, and healthcare, for different organizations across the world. She has hands-on experience working with architecture design, performance tuning, security implementation, integration, and the orchestration of complex workflows in Alfresco.

She has more than 7 years of experience in software engineering. Her journey in this field began when she started working with different open source technologies and found them interesting. She holds a bachelors of engineering degree in information technology from Gujarat University, India.

Vandana has also coauthored *Alfresco 4 Enterprise Content Management Implementation*.

I am grateful to Packt for providing this opportunity. I appreciate the guidance and help provided by Mayur Pawanikar while writing the book. Finally, I would like to thank my parents for always supporting and motivating me.

About the Reviewers

Johnny Gee is the Director of Process Automation Solutions at Flatirons Solutions, Inc. In his role, he is responsible for architecting case management solutions for multiple clients across various industries. He has over 18 years of experience in the design and implementation of the ECM system, with a proven record of successful project implementations.

In addition to earning his undergraduate degree in aerospace engineering from the University of Maryland, Johnny achieved two graduate degrees: one in aerospace engineering from Georgia Institute of Technology and the other in information systems technology from George Washington University.

Johnny is an EMC-proven professional specialist in the application and development of content management, and he helped coauthor the EMC Documentum Server Programming certification exam. He has been invited to speak at both EMC World and Alfresco Summit.

Flatirons offers content lifecycle management solutions and services across a number of industries. Its solutions include enterprise software along with consulting and implementation services to help its clients identify, develop, and deploy the best solutions suited to their needs.

Johnny was the technical reviewer of Martin Bergljung's *Alfresco 3 Business Solutions* and Munwar Shariff's *Alfresco 3 Web Content Management*. He was also the technical reviewer for Pawan Kumar's *Documentum Content Management Foundations: EMC Proven Professional Certification Exam E20-120 Study Guide*.

Piergiorgio Lucidi works at Sourcesense as a technology master of enterprise information management. Sourcesense is a European open source systems integrator, providing consultancy, support, and other services for key open source technologies.

He is also an Alfresco Certified Instructor (ACI), Alfresco Certified Engineer (ACE), and Alfresco Certified Administrator (ACA).

He works as a mentor, technical leader, and software engineer and has 12 years of experience in the areas of enterprise content management (ECM), web content management (WCM), business process management (BPM), and system integrations. He is an expert at integrating EIM and ECM solutions in web applications as well as portal applications.

He regularly contributes to the Alfresco community as a global forum moderator and Alfresco wiki gardener, and during the Alfresco DevCon 2012 in Berlin, he was named an Alfresco Community Star.

He contributes to the Apache Software Foundation as a mentor, PMC member, and committer of Apache ManifoldCF, and he is the project leader of the CMIS, Alfresco, and ElasticSearch connectors. He is a project leader and committer of the JBoss community, and he contributed to some of the projects around the JBoss Portal/GateIn platform.

He is a speaker at conferences dedicated to Java, Spring Framework, open source products, and technologies related to the ECM and WCM world.

He is an author, technical reviewer, and affiliate partner at Packt Publishing. He wrote the technical books Alfresco 3 Web Services and GateIn Cookbook.

As technical reviewer, he has also contributed to books such as *Alfresco 3 Cookbook*, *Alfresco Share*, *Alfresco 4 Enterprise Content Management*, and *Learning Alfresco Web Scripts*.

As an affiliate partner, he also writes book reviews on his website, Open4Dev (`http://www.open4dev.com/`).

I would like to thank Packt Publishing for another great opportunity to contribute to a project dedicated to the Alfresco platform.

Giuseppe Urso is a software engineer with more than 10 years of extensive work experience in design and the agile development of service-oriented applications and distributed systems based on Java SE and Java EE.

He works in the IT industry as a senior systems architect and Java developer, handling responsibilities involving architecture design and the implementation of several large-scale projects based on Alfresco ECM and Liferay Portal.

He is an Alfresco Certified Administrator (ACA) and committer on the Alfresco-SDK project. His major areas of expertise include Amazon Web Services (AWS), Elastic Compute Cloud (EC2) technologies, and Message-Oriented Middleware (MOM).

Giuseppe earned his master's degree in computer engineering from the University of Salento, Italy. He is a licensed engineer and member of the professional engineers' association called Ordine degli Ingegneri della Provincia di Lecce.

He was the technical reviewer of the book *Liferay 6.x Portal Enterprise Intranets Cookbook* by *Packt Publishing*.

As an open source enthusiast, he share on Github, projects which make use of Java Cryptography Architecture (JCA), Apache ActiveMQ and Amazon AWS technologies (`https://github.com/giuseppeurso-eu?tab=repositories`).

He runs a personal blog at www.giuseppeurso.eu where he writes articles and useful guidelines on Java, Alfresco, Liferay, and practices of GNU/Linux systems administration.

www.PacktPub.com

eBooks, discount offers, and more

Did you know that Packt offers eBook versions of every book published, with PDF and ePub files available? You can upgrade to the eBook version at `www.PacktPub.com` and as a print book customer, you are entitled to a discount on the eBook copy. Get in touch with us at `customercare@packtpub.com` for more details.

At `www.PacktPub.com`, you can also read a collection of free technical articles, sign up for a range of free newsletters and receive exclusive discounts and offers on Packt books and eBooks.

`https://www2.packtpub.com/books/subscription/packtlib`

Do you need instant solutions to your IT questions? PacktLib is Packt's online digital book library. Here, you can search, access, and read Packt's entire library of books.

Why subscribe?

- Fully searchable across every book published by Packt
- Copy and paste, print, and bookmark content
- On demand and accessible via a web browser

Table of Contents

Preface

This book focuses on the administration part of Alfresco. It also gives you a high-level understanding of Alfresco and its capabilities from the perspective of its architecture. This book provides you with details of how to administer and troubleshoot problems in Alfresco. It also gives you an in-depth insight into configuration, clustering, backup recovery, and maintenance. You thoroughly understand Alfresco's repository structure and learn how to install, configure, search, and administrate Alfresco.

What this book covers

Chapter 1, Understanding Alfresco, gives you a thorough understanding of Alfresco's architecture and its features.

Chapter 2, Setting Up the Alfresco Environment, explains the various installation processes of Alfresco in different application servers. It also provides details of best practices and troubleshooting for the environment setup.

Chapter 3, Alfresco Configuration, explains the ways in which Alfresco can be configured to suit business needs. It gives you a detailed understanding of the different components of Alfresco and how they can be configured.

Chapter 4, Administration of Alfresco, explains how the Alfresco repository can be administered. It provides you with detailed steps for the administration of the repository and the functions it can perform. The chapter gives you a thorough understanding of the administration console, users and group creation processes, node browsers, and so on.

Chapter 5, Search, focuses on the search component of Alfresco. It will provide you with a detailed insight into the installation, configuration, troubleshooting, and maintenance of the search server Solr.

Chapter 6, Permissions and Security, explores the details of the permissions required in the Alfresco repository. It provides you with an understanding about the different types of permissions and roles in Alfresco and how to integrate with different third-party authentication tools.

Chapter 7, High Availability in Alfresco, explores the different ways in which the Alfresco system can be made highly available. It covers the different methods of clustering Alfresco and its backup and recovery process as well as troubleshooting Alfresco's clustered environment.

Chapter 8, The Basics of the Alfresco Content Store, explains how Alfresco actually stores content. The content life cycle is discussed in detail in this chapter as well as the database structure in Alfresco.

Chapter 9, Maintenance and Troubleshooting, covers how to monitor and manage the Alfresco system in production using JMX and other tools. It also provides details about different ways to troubleshoot Alfresco. You will also learn about different audit trails in Alfresco for the purpose of better administration.

Chapter 10, Upgrade, explains how Alfresco can be upgraded from one version to another. It provides detailed steps in order to understand the process of upgrading.

What you need for this book

The hardware/software requirements are as follows:

- The Alfresco 5.x installer
- Tomcat
- JBoss
- A Windows/Linux operating system.

Who this book is for

The target audience includes users with a basic knowledge of content management systems and those of you who want to understand Alfresco from an administration perspective and a high-level design perspective.

Conventions

In this book, you will find a number of text styles that distinguish between different kinds of information. Here are some examples of these styles and an explanation of their meaning.

Code words in text, database table names, folder names, filenames, file extensions, pathnames, dummy URLs, user input, and Twitter handles are shown as follows: "Execute the downloaded `.bin` file."

A block of code is set as follows:

```
<module xmlns="urn:jboss:module:1.0"
name="org.alfresco.configuration">
```

When we wish to draw your attention to a particular part of a code block, the relevant lines or items are set in bold:

```
<resources>
    <resource-root path="."/>
</resources>
```

Any command-line input or output is written as follows:

```
sudo apt-get install mysql-server
sudo service mysql start|stop|status
```

New terms and **important words** are shown in bold. Words that you see on the screen, for example, in menus or dialog boxes, appear in the text like this: "There are two mode of installation: **Easy** and **Advanced**."

> Warnings or important notes appear in a box like this.

> Tips and tricks appear like this.

Reader feedback

Feedback from our readers is always welcome. Let us know what you think about this book—what you liked or disliked. Reader feedback is important for us as it helps us develop titles that you will really get the most out of.

To send us general feedback, simply e-mail `feedback@packtpub.com`, and mention the book's title in the subject of your message.

If there is a topic that you have expertise in and you are interested in either writing or contributing to a book, see our author guide at `www.packtpub.com/authors`.

Customer support

Now that you are the proud owner of a Packt book, we have a number of things to help you to get the most from your purchase.

Downloading the example code

You can download the example code files for this book from your account at `http://www.packtpub.com`. If you purchased this book elsewhere, you can visit `http://www.packtpub.com/support` and register to have the files e-mailed directly to you.

You can download the code files by following these steps:

1. Log in or register to our website using your e-mail address and password.
2. Hover the mouse pointer on the **SUPPORT** tab at the top.
3. Click on **Code Downloads & Errata**.
4. Enter the name of the book in the **Search** box.
5. Select the book for which you're looking to download the code files.
6. Choose from the drop-down menu where you purchased this book from.
7. Click on **Code Download**.

You can also download the code files by clicking on the **Code Files** button on the book's webpage at the Packt Publishing website. This page can be accessed by entering the book's name in the **Search** box. Please note that you need to be logged in to your Packt account.

Once the file is downloaded, please make sure that you unzip or extract the folder using the latest version of:

- WinRAR / 7-Zip for Windows
- Zipeg / iZip / UnRarX for Mac
- 7-Zip / PeaZip for Linux

Downloading the color images of this book

We also provide you with a PDF file that has color images of the screenshots/diagrams used in this book. The color images will help you better understand the changes in the output. You can download this file from `http://www.packtpub.com/sites/default/files/downloads/Alfresco_for_Administrators_ColoredImages.pdf`.

Errata

Although we have taken every care to ensure the accuracy of our content, mistakes do happen. If you find a mistake in one of our books—maybe a mistake in the text or the code—we would be grateful if you could report this to us. By doing so, you can save other readers from frustration and help us improve subsequent versions of this book. If you find any errata, please report them by visiting `http://www.packtpub.com/submit-errata`, selecting your book, clicking on the **Errata Submission Form** link, and entering the details of your errata. Once your errata are verified, your submission will be accepted and the errata will be uploaded to our website or added to any list of existing errata under the Errata section of that title.

To view the previously submitted errata, go to `https://www.packtpub.com/books/content/support` and enter the name of the book in the search field. The required information will appear under the **Errata** section.

Piracy

Piracy of copyrighted material on the Internet is an ongoing problem across all media. At Packt, we take the protection of our copyright and licenses very seriously. If you come across any illegal copies of our works in any form on the Internet, please provide us with the location address or website name immediately so that we can pursue a remedy.

Please contact us at `copyright@packtpub.com` with a link to the suspected pirated material.

We appreciate your help in protecting our authors and our ability to bring you valuable content.

Questions

If you have a problem with any aspect of this book, you can contact us at `questions@packtpub.com`, and we will do our best to address the problem.

1

Understanding Alfresco

Alfresco is one of the leading open source **enterprise content management systems (ECM)**. For more details about ECM refer to the Wiki; `https://en.wikipedia.org/wiki/Enterprise_content_management`. Alfresco allows you to manage content in a simple and smart way. It provides enterprise solutions based on open standards, and open source technologies for managing business critical content. As it is a very stable player in the market and provides enterprise-level features and support, Alfresco has been named *Visionary* by **Gartner** for five years in a row. Gartner is a leading research company, which provides insight into technology; refer to `http://www.gartner.com/technology/about.jsp` for more details about Gartner.

This chapter provides you with an introduction to Alfresco 5.x, its features, and its benefits. It helps you to understand the main building blocks of Alfresco.

By the end of this chapter, you will have learned about:

- An overview of Alfresco
- Key features of Alfresco
- Alfresco architecture
- Using Alfresco for your ECM requirements

Overview of Alfresco

The Alfresco open source ECM system was founded by John Newton, co-founder of Documentum, and John Powell, former COO of Business Objects, in 2005. Alfresco is a very scalable and extensible solution. Alfresco comes in various flavors: **Alfresco Enterprise Edition**, **Alfresco Community Edition**, and **Alfresco in Cloud**.

Alfresco Community Edition is only for small-scale development or research purposes. It is not recommended for production systems as there are certain functional differences. The Community version doesn't support clustering, enterprise application servers such as WebLogic, enterprise databases such as Oracle, encryption of content stores, advanced admin tools, advanced media management, and so on. There is no Alfresco support provided for the Community version. Alfresco Enterprise Edition is production-ready code. It has been load tested and certified for use in production. The Enterprise build is fully supported by Alfresco. Alfresco in Cloud is a **SaaS** (**Software as a Service**) version of Alfresco. More details on this are given in later sections.

Refer to the following URL for more details about the differences between Community and Enterprise versions:

`https://wiki.alfresco.com/wiki/Enterprise_EditionAlfresco`

Enterprise Edition has various unique features, which distinguish it from other ECM systems.

Enterprise and open source

As Alfresco is built upon open source technologies, it reduces the cost of overall software acquisition, development, and maintenance. Due to this open source model, Alfresco can use the best open source technologies on the market and build a strong system at a low cost. Alfresco provides a very cost-effective solution.

Scalable

Scalability is a very important aspect for any ECM system. For enterprise organizations in fields such as media, healthcare, finance, and so on, the amount of content grows exponentially, so scalability becomes an important parameter. As Alfresco is built using open source standards and technologies, it provides a very scalable architecture.

Alfresco Enterprise can be deployed on any platform, and supports multiple databases such as MySQL, Oracle, PostgreSQL, and so on. It also supports multiple application servers such as Tomcat, JBoss, WebLogic, and so on. Each tier in an Alfresco application can be deployed on a separate machine, which allows the vertical scalability of the system. Alfresco supports a clustered environment, which allows it to scale horizontally.

Rich media support

ECM systems should support any type of content, regardless of application or organization. Alfresco supports the storage and management of multiple types of electronic content, from normal documents to any multimedia files. It provides automatic extraction of the information from files, associates it as metadata with content, and enables easy searching.

Secured system

Security and content protection is critical for any ECM system. Alfresco has a very strong authentication and authorization model. It provides an out-of-the-box database membership system; it can also be integrated with identity management systems like **LDAP** and **Active Directory** (**AD**), and have centralized security and single sign-on. Alfresco provides full access control on individual content to ensure that security and business integrity is maintained. Access control can be set at the folder level or individual content.

Highly extensible

Because of its open source model, Alfresco can be extended and customized as per requirements. Organizations can have a trained in-house team to maintain and customize Alfresco as per their needs.

External integration

Alfresco supports open standard protocols for integration with external systems. Alfresco can be integrated with any Java-based portal, such as **Liferay** (`https://www.liferay.com/products/liferay-portal/overview`) using the **CMIS** or **REST** protocols.

CMIS is a standard open source protocol to allow a document management repository to connect with a web application. It defines an abstract layer so the web interface can connect with any repository. For more details, refer to `https://en.wikipedia.org/wiki/Content_Management_Interoperability_Services`.

The REST protocol allows an external application to access the repository using the HTTP protocol using the same HTTP verbs, such as GET, POST, and so on. For more details, refer to `https://en.wikipedia.org/wiki/Representational_state_transfer`.

Alfresco provides integration with various scanning solutions, such as **Ephesoft** or **Kofax**, which gives a complete end-to-end solution. It allows organizations to perform document capture, extraction, classification, storage, and distribution via a centralized environment.

For more details about Ephesoft and Kofax refer to these URLs:

- `http://ephesoft.com/products`
- `https://en.wikipedia.org/wiki/Kofax`

Collaboration

Nowadays, due to social media, collaboration has become very important for any organization as part of ECM. Alfresco, as well as content management, also provides a platform for collaboration between users internally and externally with full security and control over content. Powerful tools such as blogs, wikis, forums, and so on are provided within the Alfresco system to provide collaboration within teams.

Each project can have its own space for complete collaboration and the sharing of content.

Alfresco supports the publishing of content to various social platforms such as **Twitter**, **Facebook**, **YouTube**, **SlideShare**, and so on. It also provides Google Doc integration, which allows users to have real-time collaboration.

Business process management

Efficient business processes are an integral part of any organization. Automation of this process helps organizations to streamline processes, improve efficiency, and reduce cost. In organizations where the review and approval process of any document is very important, there would always be a need for these documents to be moved and accessed effectively.

Alfresco provides the Java-based, highly configurable BPM engine Activiti (`http://www.activiti.org/`). It also provides graphical tools so that less technical persons can easily design the process flow, allowing the faster rollout of processes.

As Alfresco can be accessed by any supported browser or mobile device, users get the flexibility to perform their tasks from anywhere.

Alfresco provides easy configurable rules, which can help to trigger and control this business process in a smart way.

Cloud-based ECM

Alfresco provides a fully managed SaaS ECM solution, leveraging the power of a cloud-based environment. Alfresco in Cloud is a ready-to-go Alfresco implementation which requires no installation and minimal configuration by customers. It allows full control over, and collaboration on, documents, similar to what can be achieved by Alfresco deployed on-premises.

Alfresco also supports a hybrid model, where content can be synchronized from your on-premises Alfresco to the cloud. This allows content to be always in sync and easily available from any location. An Alfresco on-premises solution can be used for long-term storage and compliance, and Alfresco in cloud can be used for sharing and collaboration too.

Search

Finding the correct content within a system is very important for any content management system. Alfresco provides searching with **Apache Solr** (`http://lucene.apache.org/solr`). It provides full-text indexing of content, and metadata indexing, which allows users to easily search and locate the content in the repository. Alfresco also provides advanced search capabilities.

Alfresco also supports searches for archived content, users, and groups in the system.

Version control

Maintaining all versions of a document is also a critical aspect of an ECM system. Alfresco provides strong version management for documents. It maintains all the version changes of a document and its associated metadata. Alfresco also has a feature that allows you to revert a document to any version.

Auditing

Alfresco provides very strong auditing. Each and every action on content is captured in an audit trail. This audit information can be easily retrieved and generated as a report.

Alfresco architecture overview

Alfresco is the leading open source option for ECM. Alfresco architecture is designed based on open standards JSR-170, JSR-168, and JSR-283. **JSRs** are industry standards defined by the Java community for uniform repository access, using the Java platform application programming interface. Refer to `https://en.wikipedia.org/wiki/Content_repository_API_for_Java` for more details.

Alfresco supports pluggable aspect-oriented architecture. It is lightweight, modular, and scalable.

The following is a high-level diagram of the Alfresco architecture:

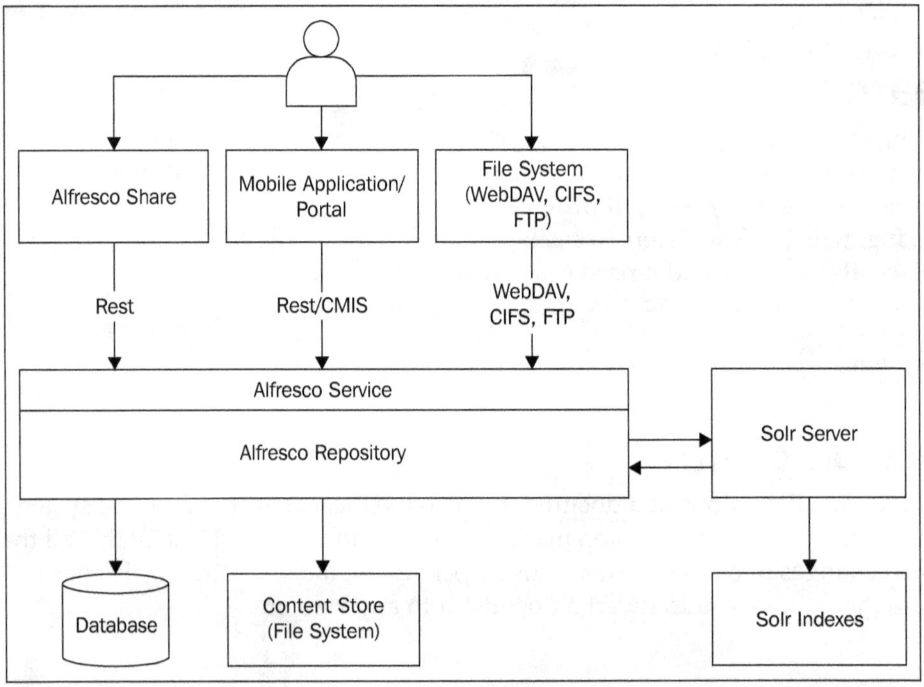
Alfresco Share
Mobile Application/ Portal
File System (WebDAV, CIFS, FTP)
Rest
Rest/CMIS
WebDAV, CIFS, FTP
Alfresco Service
Alfresco Repository
Solr Server
Database
Content Store (File System)
Solr Indexes

Alfresco Share

This is the collaboration content management platform in Alfresco. It is built on the **Surf** framework. The Surf framework was developed by Alfresco, but in 2009 Alfresco began working with Spring Source and announced the Spring Surf Extension framework. Later on, both Spring Source and Alfresco were collectively developed and are available as plugins in Spring MVC 3.x.

Refer to the following links for more details:

- `https://wiki.alfresco.com/wiki/Spring_Surf`
- `http://www.springsurf.org/`

Alfresco Share simplifies document capturing and sharing, and the retrieval of data for teams, resulting in better collaboration. This in turn increases the productivity of teams and reduces the volume of e-mails.

Alfresco Share also provides advanced administrative tools. It supports module-based extension, which supports the ability to remove, add, or modify any component without changing any out-of-the box code.

Alfresco repository

This is the main core of Alfresco. Alfresco repository is a bundle of service implementations based on the open standards of CMIS and JCR. This service provides cutting edge content management features such as:

- Content storage
- Content retrieval
- Content modeling
- Query interface
- Access control
- Audit
- Versioning

These services provide a public interface based on REST/CMIS or Java JSR-170 protocol standards which allows the client application to communicate with the repository. Alfresco Share communicates with the repository using the REST interface.

The content repository is more than a normal database application, due to the level of control over individual content it provides. Access to content is wrapped by a security layer which prevents any unauthorized access. The fine-grained security control requires a more complex approach than a traditional database application.

In Alfresco, the actual binary stream of content is located in the file system. The file folder structure and reference to this binary stream is maintained in the database.

Filesystem protocol (CIFS/WebDAV/FTP)

Access to content stored in a repository is very important for any ECM. Alfresco supports various protocols, such as **CIFS (Common Internet File System)**, WebDAV, and FTP.

These protocols allow you to support the mapping of the same file folder structure as the repository to a virtual filesystem. With these protocols, any tool that can read and write a filesystem can read and write to an Alfresco repository. Users can still use Alfresco as a locally mapped network filesystem. CIFS provides advanced compatibility with the mapped operation system. With the CIFS protocol, Windows users can use the Windows offline synchronization feature with an Alfresco repository. These virtual filesystem protocols allow users to edit and view content using their locally installed tools.

Database

The database holds all the content related information, such as metadata, content association, content binary stream location reference, and folder structure. The database also stores information related to users, workflow tasks, audits, and so on.

Alfresco supports various database vendors, such as MySQL, PostgreSQL, Oracle, and so on. Oracle is only supported in Alfresco Enterprise Edition. Database schema and more information will be covered in *Chapter 8, The Basics of the Alfresco Content Store*.

Content store

The content store is a term used for the filesystem location where the actual binary stream of content is stored. In Alfresco, only the reference to the content is stored in the database. The actual content is stored in a filesystem. This filesystem can be any normal NAS or SAN mounted drive. This architecture allows Alfresco storage to grow exponentially and makes Alfresco scalable.

Solr indexes

Searching is a very important aspect of any ECM system. Alfresco supports searches using Apache Solr. All content, metadata, and permissions associated with content in Alfresco are indexed in Solr, which allows fast searches and access to content stored in a repository.

Solr can be bundled with Alfresco on the same machine, or it can be installed as a separate tier. This design allows the horizontal scalability of the search tier. Alfresco and Solr communicate with each other asynchronously.

Business use cases of Alfresco

Alfresco as a true ECM system provides a simple and smart way to manage your content. Alfresco provides various systems as solutions to support document management, record management, collaboration, and so on, in order to solve organizational challenges.

Alfresco as a document management solution

Alfresco can be used as a document management solution for any organization where the documents are business critical, and storing and retrieving them effectively is very important for the business. For example, contracts are very important documents for many firms. All contracts can be stored in a central location within Alfresco. Strong access control can be applied to each contract document, so only authorized users can view/edit the contract.

Metadata information from the contract document can be extracted and indexed in Alfresco, which allows users to search any contract easily. As Alfresco supports full-text searches, users can search the contract document based on its content. The versioning features of Alfresco can be leveraged to ensure that all the versions of the contract are kept.

Alfresco provides a strong audit trail, so all the actions taken on the contract by any user can be captured and an audit report can be generated from them very easily.

Alfresco also supports integration with various scanning and OCR solutions, such as Ephesoft, so any paper contracts can be scanned, classified, and stored in the repository.

For contracts, the review and approval process is very important. Alfresco has strong business process management which can be leveraged to automate this process, reduce the length of the approval cycle, and improve efficiency. As Alfresco can be accessed from the Web, users can view documents and perform operations from any location.

Alfresco as a record management solution

Alfresco record management is a great solution for any organization where compliance is important. It is simple and very user-friendly. Users can adopt this system easily.

It can be extended to create a single centralized repository to manage all kinds of electronic records. Alfresco provides strong access control, so all records are secure. The policies for record use, storage, and disposal can be easily defined with Alfresco record management.

Alfresco record management is designed based on United States Department of Defence 5015.2 record management standards.

With Alfresco, you can easily drag and drop records into the system. Business rules can be defined to classify and mark them as records. A disposition policy can be defined and automated, which includes the transfer of records or their complete destruction after a given period. In addition to this, there is strong auditing that captures all actions on the records.

Alfresco provides different reports that show recent records, records due for expiry, records due for destruction, and records due for transfer.

Alfresco for collaboration

Alfresco can be used in collaboration solutions within an organization, along with content management. For example, a marketing team can work on different projects. Alfresco Share can be used as a collaboration platform. Each marketing project can be created as a different space. Only members of that project can have access to that space.

Teams can upload, share, and discuss content within this space. There are dashboards which can be configured as per user needs to see the activity in the project and notifications. Alfresco acts as a central repository to manage all types of marketing documents.

Alfresco provides a feature for publishing content to any social platform, including Twitter, SlideShare, and Facebook, which can be leveraged and content can be published directly.

With Alfresco, content can be shared with external users in a secure and controlled way.

For more case studies on Alfresco, you can refer to `http://www.alfresco.com/customers`.

Summary

Alfresco is one of the leading open source ECM systems. The key features of Alfresco are security, stability, and a scalable architecture. Due to its open source model, Alfresco can use the best open source technologies on the market and build a strong system at a low cost. Alfresco provides a very cost effective solution.

Alfresco architecture is designed based on JCR open standards. It is lightweight, modular, and scalable.

Alfresco can be used in the cloud, on-premises, or as a hybrid. The next chapter will cover details about the installation of an Alfresco system on various platforms.

2

Setting Up the Alfresco Environment

Alfresco provides users with a very flexible mechanism for installation. Alfresco can be installed on any supported application server like **Tomcat**, **JBoss**, **WebLogic**, and so on. Alfresco also supports various databases. Different components of Alfresco can be separated out or installed together on the same machine, so you can pick your package based on organization needs and do the setup.

In this chapter, we will cover the different installation processes of Alfresco:

- Understanding the installation process using the installer file with a simple wizard
- Diving into detailed steps for the manual installation of Alfresco in Tomcat
- The installation process of Alfresco in the JBoss application server

Here, the main focus is on the installation process of Alfresco; we are not covering topics related to the installation of databases or other components.

Installing Alfresco using a wizard

Alfresco provides users with different installer files for its setup based on the different OS platforms. This installation file provides a complete package bundle like Tomcat, Java, PostgreSQL, Solr, LibreOffice. It is a simple wizard-based process for installation.

Let's go through the installation process in detail:

1. The first step is to download the proper installer based on the operating system required for Alfresco setup. Here, we are using the example of the Windows 64 bit system. For Windows 64 bit, download `alfresco-enterprise-5.x.x.x-installer-win-x64.bin`. Refer to `https://www.alfresco.com/services/subscription/supported-platforms` to identify the Alfresco supported platforms. Alfresco Enterprise can be downloaded from `https://myalfresco.force.com/support`, but only if you have Enterprise access. A 30 day trial version can be downloaded from the Alfresco portal after submitting a form. A community version can also be downloaded from the Alfresco portal or any public websites like SourceForge.
2. Execute the downloaded `.bin` file. If you are on Linux make sure you have granted executable permission to the installer file.
3. Select the appropriate language, as shown in the following screenshot:

Language Selection
Please select the installation language
English - English
OK
Cancel

4. There are two modes of installation: **Easy** and **Advanced**. The **Easy** mode installs Alfresco with the default configuration. In **Advanced** mode, you can specify port details for all required components. It's better to select the **Advanced** mode.

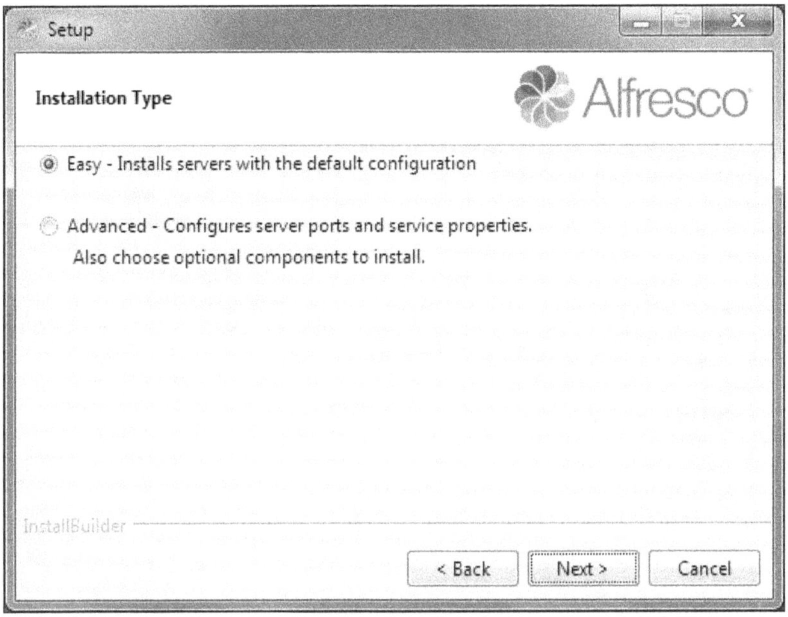
Setup
Installation Type
Alfresco
Easy - Installs servers with the default configuration
Advanced - Configures server ports and service properties.
Also choose optional components to install.
InstallBuilder
< Back
Next >
Cancel

5. Let's select the advanced configuration. In the next window, you will get a list of all the components required for installation. You can check or uncheck the components based on your needs. For example, if you have installed PostgreSQL independently, then uncheck PostgreSQL. If you uncheck, make sure you can configure those properly after installation is complete.

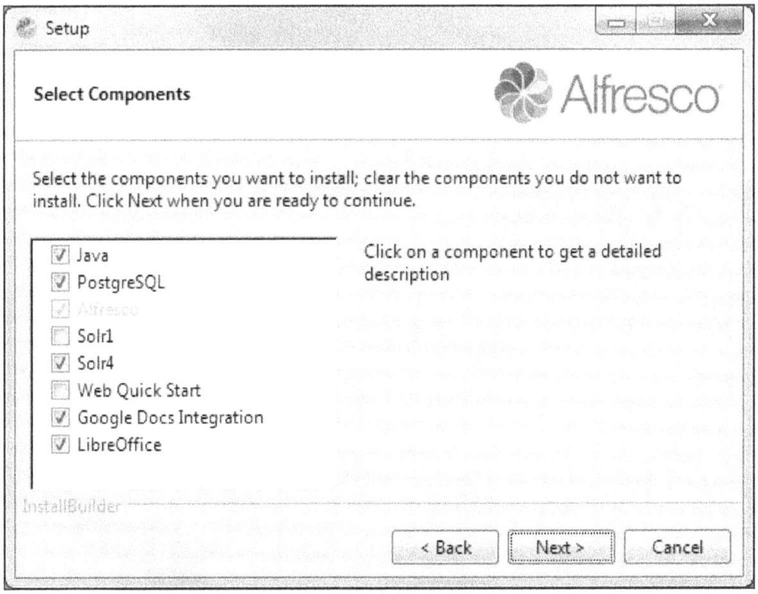
Setup
Select Components
Alfresco
Select the components you want to install; clear the components you do not want to install. Click Next when you are ready to continue.
Java
PostgreSQL
Alfresco
Solr1
Solr4
Web Quick Start
Google Docs Integration
LibreOffice
Click on a component to get a detailed description
InstallBuilder
< Back
Next >
Cancel

6. The next step is to provide the root folder name where Alfresco will be installed, as shown in the following screenshot. You can browse and also select a directory by using the browse icon next to the text box.

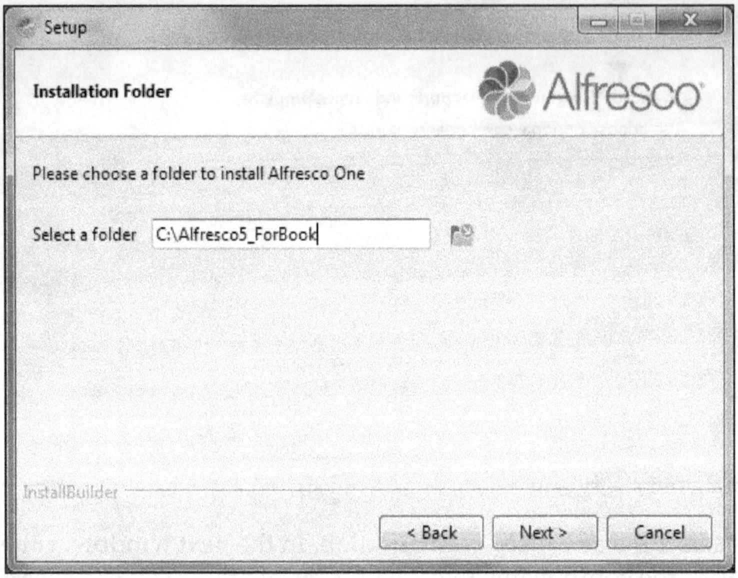
Setup
Installation Folder
Alfresco
Please choose a folder to install Alfresco One
Select a folder
C:\Alfresco5_ForBook
InstallBuilder
< Back
Next >
Cancel

7. Later, we provide the database port number. If you already have another instance of PostgreSQL running, you have to provide a different port number. The default is set to `5432`.

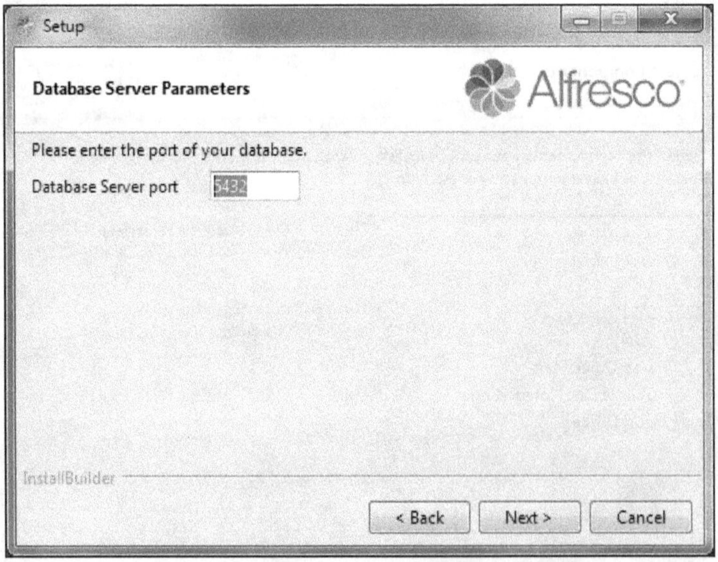
Setup
Database Server Parameters
Alfresco
Please enter the port of your database.
Database Server port
5432
InstallBuilder
< Back
Next >
Cancel

8. In addition to database configuration, the Tomcat server also requires port configuration for startup, shutdown, and SSL ports, as shown in the screenshot below. By default, the text boxes are filled with the default values as shown below. If you have any other application running on the same ports, change the port appropriately. Also make sure that the ports you are providing are open in your firewall.

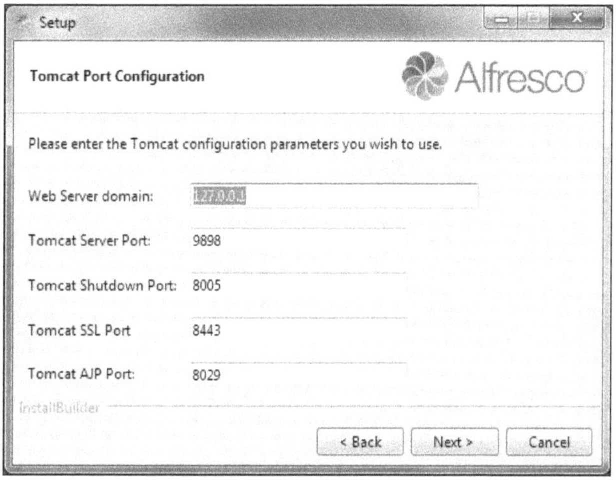
Setup
Tomcat Port Configuration
Alfresco
Please enter the Tomcat configuration parameters you wish to use.
Web Server domain: 127.0.0.1
Tomcat Server Port: 9898
Tomcat Shutdown Port: 8005
Tomcat SSL Port 8443
Tomcat AJP Port: 8029
InstallBuilder
< Back
Next >
Cancel

9. Alfresco requires a remote RMI port configuration. By default, it is set to `50500`, but if you have another Alfresco instance running on the same RMI port, make sure this port is changed. Make sure this port is open through your firewall. **RMI** means **Remote Method Invocation**, and certain Alfresco services are exposed via RMI in Alfresco. This port is the RMI registry port, which will be used by a remote client.

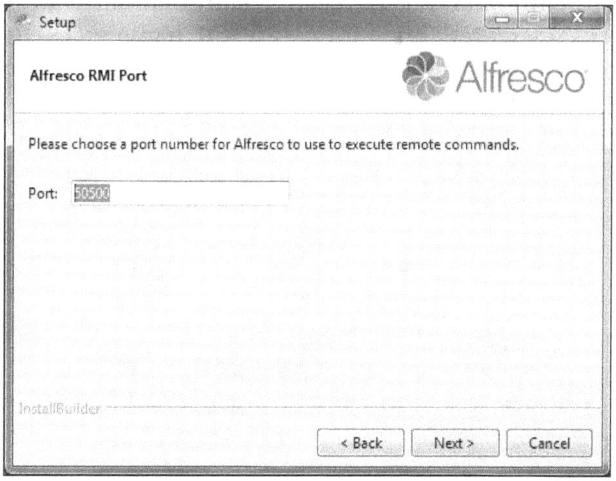
Setup
Alfresco RMI Port
Alfresco
Please choose a port number for Alfresco to use to execute remote commands.
Port: 50500
InstallBuilder
< Back
Next >
Cancel

10. Now, provide the admin credentials for the Alfresco repository. It is important that you provide strong credentials, and make sure you remember that.

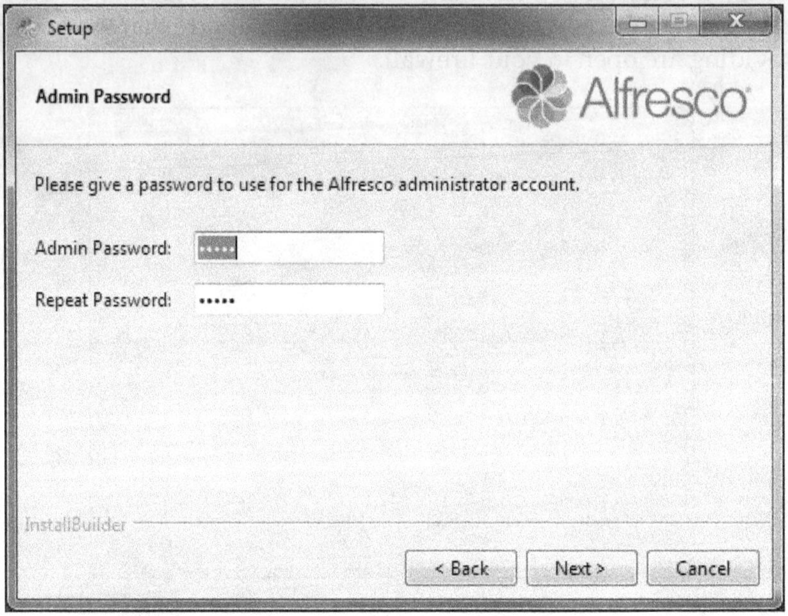
Setup
Admin Password
Alfresco
Please give a password to use for the Alfresco administrator account.
Admin Password:
Repeat Password:
InstallBuilder
< Back
Next >
Cancel

11. If you have selected to install Libre office, you can configure the port for Libre office.
12. This installation wizard sets up Alfresco as a Windows service. The last step prompts you to select the startup option for service as either manual or automatic. As the name suggests, automatic will start on reboot of the machine and with manual, you need to start manually. In Windows, there are two services created: one for PostgreSQL named `alfrescoPostgreSQL`, and one for Tomcat named `alfrescoTomcat`. If you have multiple instances, it will increment with a number.

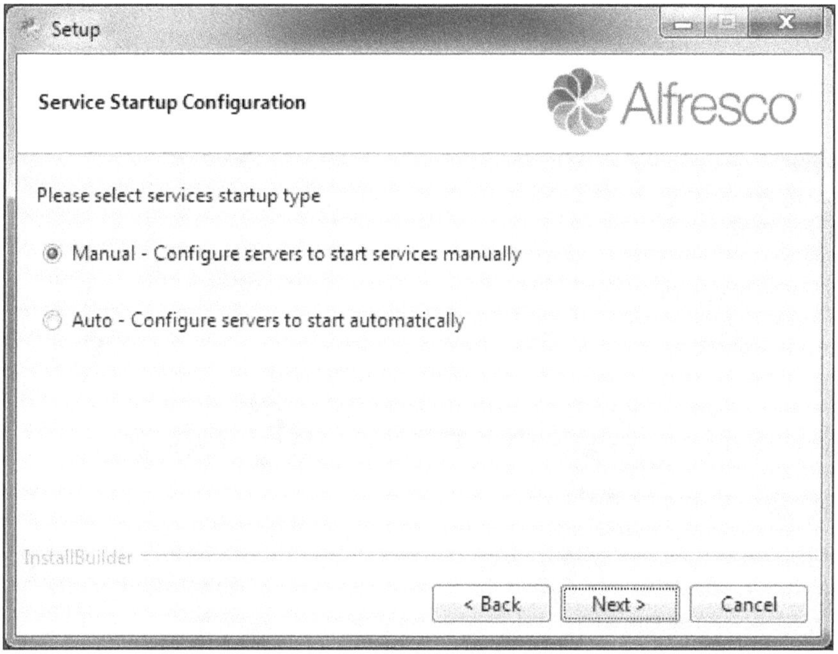
Setup
Service Startup Configuration
Alfresco
Please select services startup type
Manual - Configure servers to start services manually
Auto - Configure servers to start automatically
InstallBuilder
< Back
Next >
Cancel

13. Once all configuration information has been provided, let the installation start. Once installation is complete, it will show the finished dialog and will also ask you to open the share console.
14. You can start and stop the Alfresco server using the service. If Alfresco is installed in Linux and you cannot start it properly using the service, there is an alternative way to manually start using the `alfresco.sh` file available in the installation directory.
15. Log files are available under `<Alfresco Installation Path>/tomcat/logs`. You can monitor logs for any error in the startup process.
16. Once Alfresco is installed, there are a set of directories created under the installation path; here are some details about a few of them:
    - `solr4`: This directory contains all the configuration for Solr.
    - `alf_data`: This directory contains `contentstore` to store the binary file of the repository and Solr indexes.
    - `tomcat`: As the name suggests, this is the main Tomcat folder with all the WAR files and configuration for Alfresco and Share.
    - `postgresql`: This is the database folder for the PostgreSQL installed using the setup wizard. Under the `bin` directory, you can use the `pgAdmin3.exe` file to open the PostgreSQL user interface and connect to the Alfresco database.

17. If you are installing on Linux, make sure that the below set of libraries are installed. Based on different flavors of Linux, the commands for installation may vary:
    - `libfontconfig.so`
    - `libSM.so`
    - `libICE.so`
    - `libXrender.so`
    - `libXext.so`
    - `libXinerama.so`

Installing Alfresco manually on a Tomcat server

We went through the process of using the wizard, which installs all the required components and Alfresco as a bundle. Now if you want to install everything manually, there are some different steps required.

The very first important step will be to find out the supported stack from Alfresco. Based on the version number, decide the OS, JDK, Database, Tomcat, and other component versions required for its installation. This supported stack for the latest version of Alfresco is available on their website; `https://www.alfresco.com/services/subscription/supported-platforms`.

Once you have the supported stack and decided on the version, prepare the server for Alfresco installation:

1. Install the supported JDK, Database , Imagemagick, LibreOffice, Ghostscript, and application server for Tomcat (assuming you are using this).
2. Based on the Alfresco support stack for Alfresco 5, we need Java 7 or Java8. For example, if we need to install Java 7 on Linux OS, one way to do so can be found in the steps listed below. You can also install Oracle JDK by downloading and extracting the `tar.gz` file or `rpm` package. Download Java 7 at the following location: `http://www.oracle.com/technetwork/java/javase/downloads/jre7-downloads-1880261.html`

```
sudo add-apt-repository ppa:webupd8team/java
sudo apt-get update
sudo apt-get install oracle-java7-installer
```

> Note: For installation in Linux, you need either root access or sudo access on the server.

3. Once Oracle Java is installed, make sure the environment variable `JAVA_HOME` is set correctly to point to the proper Java location. Verify the `/etc/environment` file. Execute the command below to verify the Java version:

   ```
   java -version
   ```

4. Now, we need to install the Tomcat server for Alfresco. Use the Linux comment `apt-get` to install Tomcat7. This will install Tomcat7 under the `/var/lib/` directory as a service. To view the `init` script, check the file `/etc/init.d/tomcat7`.

   ```
   sudo apt-get install tomcat7
   ```

   > Make sure the JVM settings and `JAVA_HOME` is set correctly for Tomcat by editing the file `/etc/default/tomcat7`.

   ```
   sudo vi /etc/default/tomcat7
   ```

   - Sample JVM settings:

     ```
     JAVA_HOME=/usr/lib/jvm/java-6-oracle
     JAVA_OPTS = -Xmx8g -XX:MaxPermSize=256m -
     XX:+UseConcMarkSweepGC -server
     ```

   - Start the service using the command below. Tomcat will be started using the user `tomcat7`, which is a non-root user.

     ```
     sudo service tomcat7 start
     ```

5. Libre office and other transformation tools can be installed in Linux by either using the `deb` package or by using the `.tar`, `.gz` file.
6. Install the database as per the supported stack. Let's take the MySQL database as an example. The apt-get command mentioned below is one of the ways to install the MySQL server. This will install the MySQL server as a service in Linux.

   ```
   sudo apt-get install mysql-server
   sudo service mysql start|stop|status
   ```

7. Create a blank `alfresco` database and grant all permissions to the SQL user on the database which will be used by Alfresco to connect to this database. The same credentials will be used in a later step while configuring Alfresco. Below is the sample SQL query snippet for creating an Alfresco database and also for granting all privileges to the `alfresco` user.

   ```
   Create database alfresco;
   grant all on alfresco.* to 'alfresco'@'localhost' identified by
   'alfresco' with grant option;
   grant all on alfresco.* to 'alfresco'@'localhost.localdomain'
   identified by 'alfresco' with grant option;
   ```

8. Now, once all the required components have been installed, let's proceed with the Alfresco setup. Make sure that Tomcat is not running.
9. Download the Alfresco enterprise `.zip` bundle from Alfresco support.
10. Copy the proper JDBC connector library under the `<Tomcat Home>/lib` directory. If you have a MySQL database, for Alfresco 5.0, you will require the MySQL connector file `mysql-connector-java-5.1.32-bin.jar`.
11. Create `shared/classes` and the `shared/lib` directory under the Tomcat home directory.
12. Configure `conf/catalina.properties` files in Tomcat to load the `shared/classes` and `shared/lib` directory as all Alfresco extension files will be placed in these directories. Add the `shared.loader` property in the `catalina.properties` file as shown here:

    ```
    shared.loader=${catalina.base}/shared/classes,${catalina.base}/
    shared/lib/*.jar
    ```

13. Configure `server.xml` under the `conf` directory in Tomcat. Increase the HTTP header size and encoding. The default header size won't be sufficient for Alfresco. An encoding change is required to support international characters while uploading, renaming, and other operations from Alfresco Share.

    Locate the `Connector` tag for server startup in Tomcat `server.xml` and `add/modify` the two items below:

    ```
    URIEncoding="UTF-8"
    maxHttpHeaderSize="32768"
    ```

14. Extract the Alfresco `.zip` bundle downloaded in step 4 in the proper installation directory. For example, your Tomcat server should be installed under `/opt/Alfresco/Tomcat`. Extract the zip under `/opt/Alfresco`.

15. Copy the `.war` file from `web-server/webapps` directory to the `<Tomcat Home>/webapps` directory, assuming no other application is installed on this Tomcat server.
16. Copy the files and directory in `web-server/shared` into `<Tomcat Home>/shared`.
17. Configure the `alfresco-global.properties.sample` file in your Alfresco extracted bundle under `web-server/classpath` to point to the correct database and `contentstore` location. Remove the `.sample` extension. Below is the list of important configurations to be changed. For more detail on configuration, you can refer to *Chapter 3, Alfresco Configuration* and *Chapter 4, Administration of Alfresco*. Copy the `alfresco-global.properties` file under `<TOMCAT_HOME>/shared/classes`:

```
dir.root=<Full path for contentstore >
dir.keystore=<Full path for Keystore. This will be required
    for Solr. Make sure the keystore is pointing the
    location where it was extracted from zip bundle>
db.username=<Username of the SQL user setup in step 2>
db.password=<Password of the SQL  user setup in step 2>
db.driver=<Driver information based on the database used>
db.url =<Full url for database connection>
```

18. Once Alfresco is installed, you have to generate the `keystore` for Solr and configure it accordingly in the `solr` directory. For this, get the `generate_keystores.sh` file from Alfresco support.
19. Once you have the `.sh` file, make sure `ALFRESCO_HOME`, `SOLR_HOME`, `JAVA_HOME`, `SOLR & REPO` cert name are being set properly. Once all these properties are configured, execute the script to generate the new `keystore`. It will provide you with the status message and also the `dir.keystore` value to be set in the `alfresco-global.properties` file.
20. Now start the Alfresco server and monitor the logs under the `<Tomcat Home>/logs` directory. If you are starting the Alfresco server as a non-root user in Linux, the application cannot listen on privilege ports; this can be solved using `iptables`.

Installing Alfresco in JBoss

The Alfresco application is supported in various application servers; one of the supported platforms is JBoss. Installing Alfresco on JBoss requires some additional steps to installing on Tomcat.

Similar to what we did for installing Alfresco in Tomcat, install JDK, the JBoss application server, and the database based on the supported stack and follow the steps below to deploy Alfresco in JBoss. Make sure JBoss is not running. Here, are considering PostgreSQL database.

Refer to the JBoss installation and administration guide for more details on JBoss at: `https://access.redhat.com/documentation/en-US/JBoss_Enterprise_Application_Platform/6.2/index.html`

1. Download the `alfresco-enterprise-ear-5.x.x.zip` bundle from Alfresco support and extract the `.zip` bundle under some temporary location; let's call this directory `ALFRESCO_TEMP_DEPLOYMENT` for future reference. For example, in Windows, if you have extracted Alfresco 5.0.3 within the C directory, the full path will look something like this; `C:\\ ALFRESCO_TEMP_DEPLOYMENT`. On extraction of the `.zip` file, you can see the directory structure as shown in the screenshot below:

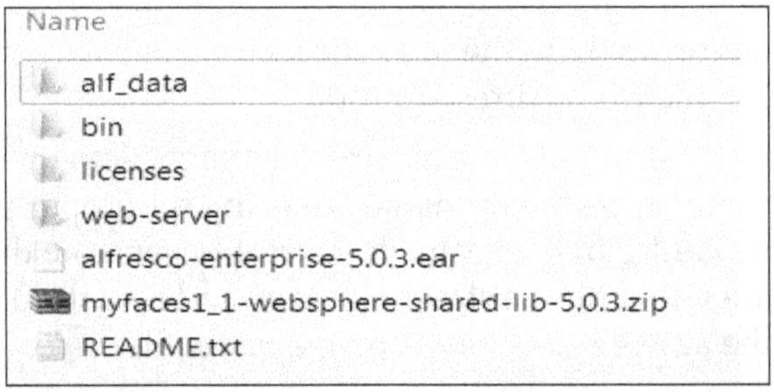
Name
alf_data
bin
licenses
web-server
alfresco-enterprise-5.0.3.ear
myfaces1_1-websphere-shared-lib-5.0.3.zip
README.txt

2. All configurations of Alfresco will go under modules of JBoss. Create a `main` directory in <JBOSS_HOME>/modules/org/alfresco/configuration.
3. Create a `module.xml` file in this `main` directory with the code snapshot below:

```
<module xmlns="urn:jboss:module:1.0"
name="org.alfresco.configuration">
<resources>
    <resource-root path="."/>
</resources>
</module>
```

4. Now copy all the files from ALFRESCO_TEMP_DEPLOYMENT/web-server/classpath, which is in the temporary folder where the .zip file was extracted, in the main directory created in step 2.

5. Configure the alfresco-global.properties.sample file under <JBOSS_HOME>/modules/org/alfresco/configuration/main, as we did in a similar way while deploying Alfresco in Tomcat. Remove the .sample extension. Don't configure anything with the database at this point. You can refer to the alfresco-global.properties file provided with the chapter. Also make sure the dir.root command should point to the proper contentstore location. Copy the alf_data directory from ALFRESCO_TEMP_DEPLOYMENT to the location where the binary file will be stored.

6. Extract the alfresco-enterprise-5.x.x.war file located in the ALFRESCO_TEMP_DEPLOYMENT directory created in step 1. You will have a set of .war files and a META-INF directory. Within META-INF, make sure the file jboss-deployment-structure.xml is set to the proper WAR configuration location, as shown here. Make sure the highlighted sections are configured properly, this is to link the configuration directory created in step 2 with the .war files.

```
<jboss-deployment-structure>
<sub-deployment name="alfresco.war">
<dependencies>
<module name="org.alfresco.configuration" />
<module name="org.apache.xalan" />
</dependencies>
</sub-deployment>
<sub-deployment name="share.war">
<dependencies>
<module name="org.alfresco.configuration" />
</dependencies>
</sub-deployment>
</jboss-deployment-structure>
```

7. Assuming we are using a PostgreSQL database, create a directory, org/postgresql/main, under the <JBOSS_HOME>/modules directory. Copy the database connector .jar in the jboss module <JBOSS HOME>/modules/org/postgresql/main directory. For a different database, refer to JBoss configuration on the JBoss website.

8. Create a `module.xml` file under the main directory for setting the PostgreSQL `.jar` location, as shown in the code snapshot below. The PostgreSQL connector `.jar` name should match with the one deployed in step 7.

```
<module xmlns="urn:jboss:module:1.0" name="org.postgresql">
  <resources>
    <resource-root path="postgresql-9.3-1102-jdbc41.jar"/>
  </resources>
  <dependencies>
    <module name="javax.api"/>
    <module name="javax.transaction.api"/>
  </dependencies>
</module>
```

9. Now you have to configure the Datasource subsystem to point to the correct database and database connector location. Configure the `standalone.xml` file located at `<JBOSS Home>/standalone/configuration`, as shown in the code snapshot below. The highlighted sections show the details to be configured. Make sure the connection URL and database credentials are configured properly. The maximum pool size should be configured based on the thread pool of the application server plus 75 more. If the thread pool size for the application server is 100, the database max connection pool size should be 175. Ensure your database is also configured accordingly. Refer to the `standalone.xml` file provided with the chapter.

```
<datasource jndi-name="java:jboss/PostgresDS" pool-
name="jbossdatasource" enabled="true">
  <connection-url>jdbc:postgresql://localhost:5432/postgresdb</
connection-url>
    <driver>postgresql</driver>
    <pool>
      <min-pool-size>0</min-pool-size>
      <max-pool-size>20</max-pool-size>
    </pool>
    <security>
      <user-name>alfresco</user-name>
      <password>admin</password>
    </security>
    <validation>
      <valid-connection-checker class-name="org.
jboss.jca.adapters.jdbc.extensions.postgres.
PostgreSQLValidConnectionChecker"/>
      <exception-sorter class-name="org.jboss.jca.adapters.jdbc.
extensions.postgres.PostgreSQLExceptionSorter"/>
    </validation>
  </datasource>
```

```
<drivers>
  <driver name="postgresql" module="org.postgresql">
    <xa-datasource-class>org.postgresql.xa.PGXADataSource</xa-
datasource-class>
  </driver>
</drivers>
```

10. Set `enable-welcome-root="false"` in the `standalone.xml` file in `<JBOSS Home>/standalone/configuration`:

```
<subsystem xmlns="urn:jboss:domain:web:1.5" default-virtual-
server="default-host" native="false">
  <connector name="http" protocol="HTTP/1.1" scheme="http" socket-
binding="http"/>
  <virtual-server name="default-host" enable-welcome-root="false">
    <alias name="localhost"/>
    <alias name="example.com"/>
  </virtual-server>
</subsystem>
```

11. Unzip the `alfresco.war` file located in the temporary directory `ALFRESCO_TEMP_DEPLOYMENT` created in step 6 on extraction of the `.ear` file. Modify the `jboss-context.xml` file in `WEB-INF` to have the proper `datasource jndi-name` reference created in step 9. Below is the highlighted code snapshot:

```
<resource-ref>
<res-ref-name>jdbc/dataSource</res-ref-name>
<jndi-name>java:jboss/PostgresDS</jndi-name>
</resource-ref>
<resource-ref>
<res-ref-name>jdbc/activitiIdGeneratorDataSource</res-ref-name>
<jndi-name>java:jboss/PostgresDS</jndi-name>
</resource-ref>
```

12. There are few issues with Java 8 and the Eclipse compiler for Java. To resolve this issue, you have to install a few additional libraries. Follow the steps below:
    - Download the ECJ4.4 `.jar` file
    - Update the `ecj` JAR location with the new `.jar` file name in `<JBOSS Home>/modules/system/layers/base/org/jboss/as/web/main/module.xml`

13. The vaadin jar file also need to be updated, so copy the vaadin-application-server-class-loader-workaround-1.0.1.jar from the ALFRESCO_TEMP_DEPLOYMENT/web-server/lib directory to the extracted alfresco.war file WEB-INF/lib created in step 11.
14. Make sure that proper memory is allocated to JBoss by configuring the standalone.conf file located at <JBOSS Home>/bin.
15. Configure the standalone.xml file located at <JBOSS Home>/standalone/configuration to set the proper URI encoding. Below is the code snapshot; add this after the extension tag. Refer to the standalone.xml file provided with this chapter.

```
<system-properties>
  <property name="org.apache.catalina.connector.URI_ENCODING"
value="UTF-8"/>
  <property name="org.apache.catalina.connector.USE_BODY_ENCODING_
FOR_QUERY_STRING" value="true"/>
</system-properties>
```

16. Disable the webservices module in JBoss by commenting out the listed extension below and subsystem tags in the standalone.xml file located at <JBOSS_HOME>/standalone/configuration.

```
  <extension module="org.jboss.as.webservices"/>

  <subsystem xmlns="urn:jboss:domain:webservices:1.2">
    ..
  </subsystem>
```

17. Enable Alfresco application logging by configuring standalone.xml. A sample log snippet is to be added within <subsystem xmlns="urn:jboss:domain:logging:1.3"> in the standalone.xml file. Refer to the standalone.xml file provided with this chapter.

```
<logger category="org.alfresco.repo.admin">
  <level name="INFO"/>
</logger>
```

18. Again, compress the extracted alfresco.war and alfresco-enterprise-5.x.x.ear files to include the changes. Start the JBoss server.

19. Open the **JBoss Management** console, add the Alfresco `.ear` file created in step 17 in **Runtime / Manage Deployments**. Click the **Enable** button and Alfresco will be deployed.

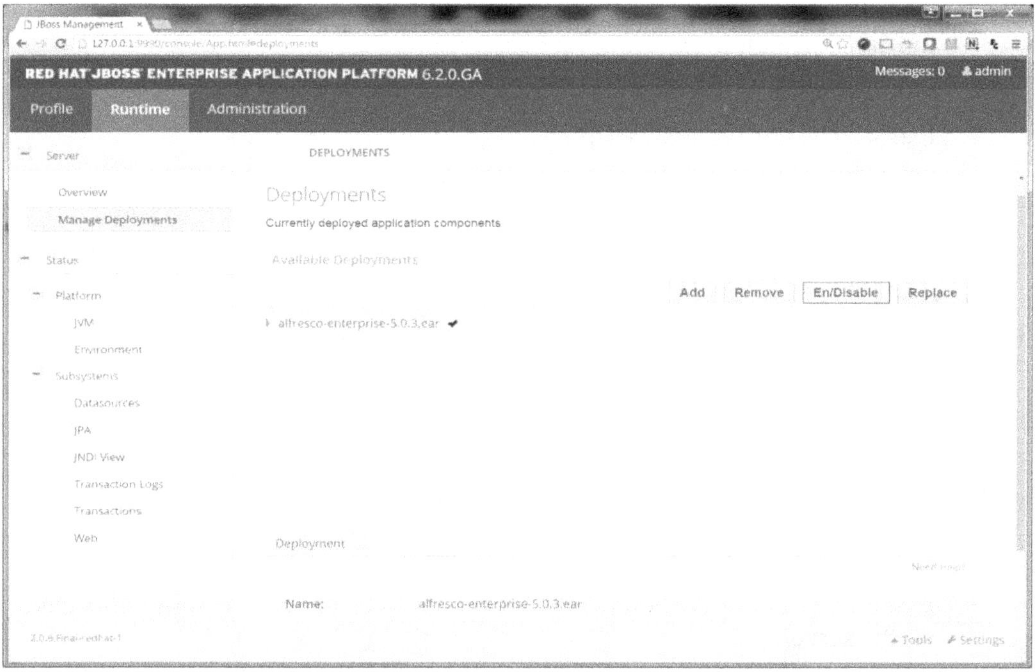
RED HAT JBOSS ENTERPRISE APPLICATION PLATFORM 6.2.0.GA
Messages: 0
admin
Profile
Runtime
Administration
Server
DEPLOYMENTS
Overview
Manage Deployments
Deployments
Currently deployed application components
Status
Available Deployments
Platform
Add
Remove
En/Disable
Replace
JVM
alfresco-enterprise-5.0.3.ear
Environment
Subsystems
Datasources
JPA
JNDI View
Transaction Logs
Transactions
Web
Deployment
Name:
alfresco-enterprise-5.0.3.ear
Tools
Settings

20. Monitor the `logs` file for any startup issues.

Installating AMP

Alfresco provides a clean mechanism to deploy extensions or patches on the existing installation using the `amp` packages. **AMP** stands for **Alfresco Module Package**. Only the changed files can be bundled together as an AMP, and each AMP is provided a proper version number.

Installing `amp` is very simple in Alfresco. Under the `<Alfresco Home>/tomcat/bin` directory, there is an `apply_amp sh` or `.bat` file based on operating system.

1. Copy the `amp` file in the `<Alfresco Home>/amps` directory if the deployment is for the Alfresco repository. If you need to deploy for Share, copy the `amp` in the `amp_share` folder.
2. Stop Alfresco.
3. Execute the `apply_amps` script.
4. Start Alfresco once the `amp` package has been applied.

Troubleshooting tips and best practices

There are few things which administrators should take care of during installation of the Alfresco server:

- Always make sure the software required for Alfresco installations are verified against the Alfresco supported stack. If you have bought an Alfresco subscription, it is recommended to raise a ticket with Alfresco support to validate your software together with your Alfresco partner and the architecture before installing it in your production environment.
- Based on your application needs, there should be enough memory allocated on the server.
- I/O operation should be fast and validate your disk performance, and it should be geographically near to the Solr instance. The filesystem used for storing Solr indexes should have great performance and should be installed in a local SSD or fiber connection.
- Validate your network; latency should not be high
- Alfresco uses many privileged ports like `25, 21,` and so on. It is recommended to manage the Alfresco application with a non-root user. Make sure there is a proper redirection set, as the default privileged ports won't work.
- The clock speed of the Alfresco machine should be greater than 2.5 GHz
- Make sure your JVM is always tuned properly based on your application requirements.
- Your database should be tuned and proper indexes should be created for tables.

- Make sure the `Temp` directory is allocated the proper size.
- The server DNS should be configured properly.
- The JVM and Alfresco installation directories should not contain spaces in their names.
- Make sure the user starting the Alfresco service is granted proper permission on the content store and Alfresco installation directory.

Refer to *Day Zero Configuration Guide* for more details about installation validation and environment configuration at `https://www.alfresco.com/cmis/browser?id=workspace%3A//SpacesStore/006ee253-2a01-4e0e-b4e8-7e74aaf5fbc7`.

Summary

In this chapter, we covered the installation processes of Alfresco. Alfresco provides a lot of flexibility during the installation process. You can either use the installer or manually install all the components. We covered the steps for installing Alfresco in the Tomcat and JBoss application servers. There are also a few tips for administrators which should be kept in mind while installing Alfresco.

In the next chapter, we will dive into the configurations of Alfresco. We will see various ways to configure the database, logging, and content store in Alfresco.

3
Alfresco Configuration

For any system, how easy it can be configured and extended is very important. Alfresco provides an easy configuration and extension mechanism. The components of Alfresco such as its database, content store location, e-mail, authentication, and so on, can very easily be configured based on business needs. Alfresco provides different ways to extend and configure the system.

This chapter will provide you with an introduction on some ways to configure Alfresco's different components and a few important configuration properties.

By the end of this chapter, you would have learned about the following:

- Understanding Alfresco configuration
- Different ways to configure Alfresco
- Steps to configure Alfresco's repository
- Understanding a subsystem

The basics of Alfresco configuration

Alfresco can be easily configured based on business needs. We can enable or disable components based on certain requirements. Alfresco exposes its configuration in its properties and an `.xml` file, which makes it easy configurable.

All the configuration files in Alfresco are in the `<configroot>` and `<configrootShare>` directory, which are within the expanded Alfresco and Share `.war` based on the application server it is deployed.

For Tomcat, these directories are:

- `<TOMCAT_HOME>/webapps/alfresco/WEB-INF/classes/alfresco`
- `<TOMbCAT_HOME>/webapps/share/WEB-INF/classes/alfresco`

The `repository.properties` file is one of the most important files which holds all the important repository configurations for a database, content store, and index. This file is moved to a JAR file in Alfresco 5.x.

Some of the important properties of Alfresco are:

- `dir.*`: This is the default configuration for the content store
- `db.*`: This is the default configuration for the database connection
- `index.*`: This is the default configuration related to indexes
- `audit.*`: This is the default configuration to turn the audit on or off as per requirements

The `.xml` configuration files in `<configroot>` and `<configShareRoot>`, such as `web-client-config.xml` and `share-config.xml`, are to configure the Alfresco Web Client and Share. The Alfresco Web Client is deprecated from version Alfresco 5.x.

Other `.xml` files are to define spring beans and configuration for all the services of the repository.

Extending configuration files

Core files should not be modified, so Alfresco provides an extension mechanism to extend/modify the system.

Configurable property files can be extended in three ways:

1. Add and modify the property in the `alfresco-global.properties` file, which is located at `<TOMCAT_HOME>/shared/classes/`.
2. Using **JMX (Java Management Extensions)**, which will be discussed in *Chapter 9, Maintenance and Troubleshooting*. JMX is Java-based technology where different components of an application can be represented as MBeans and be managed and monitored.
3. Using the Alfresco admin console, which is an independent secure page that's separate from Alfresco's Web Client and Share. This will be discussed in *Chapter 4, Administration of Alfresco.*

Option 1 would require a server restart for these changes to have effect, while option 2 and 3 can be done on the fly without a server restart.

Let's understand how a property can be modified using option 1. For example, suppose you want to disable auditing in your repository, which is enabled by default in `repository.properties`:

```
audit.enabled=true
```

Now, add and modify the following below value in `alfresco-global.properties` and restart the server. The audit will be disabled.

```
audit.enabled=false
```

To extend the `.xml` file, Alfresco also provides an extension directory. The location of the `extension` folder in the Tomcat server is as follows:

- `<TOMCAT_HOME>/shared/classes/alfresco/extension`
- `<TOMCAT_HOME>/shared/classes/alfresco/web-extension` (this is for a shared configuration extension)

You can create your own custom `context.xml` file and change the configuration for defined beans.

This will overwrite the default value. There are various sample files provided in the `extension` directory; you can refer to them for further explanation.

Configuring subsystems in Alfresco

Subsystems are individual components embedded within Alfresco. Independent functionalities are wrapped as one subsystem, for example the search functionality is wrapped as one of the subsystems in Alfresco. These packages have its own separate Spring application context and configuration files, which allows them to take control (start, stop, and configure) without affecting the main server. Multiple instances can be created for each subsystem implementation.

Some of the main subsystems are:

- Search
- Fileserver
- Authentication
- Google Docs
- E-mail
- Audit

Each subsystem has a category and type:

- **Category**: This describes the functionality of a subsystem (for example, e-mail)
- **Type**: This refers to a name of a specific implementation of a subsystem. For example, Authentication has various types of implementation such as **LDAP**, and **Kerberos**. A subsystem with a single implementation defines default as a `type`.

The default configuration of a subsystem is located at `<install_folder>\tomcat\webapps\alfresco\WEB-INF\classes\alfresco\subsystem\<category>\<type>`.

For example, all the files for the Authentication subsystem of LDAP will be located at `<install_folder>\tomcat\webapps\alfresco\WEB-INF\classes\alfresco\subsystem\Authentication\ldap`.

Each subsystem directory mainly have the `*-context.xml` and `*.properties` configuration files. These files will be loaded by the subsystem's application context.

A subsystem works as an abstract system hiding its implementation. In Alfresco, the main server accesses the subsystem by mounting it. This is achieved with the help of the declaration of bean with the `ChildApplicationContextFactory` class. An instance of this class encloses the Spring application context of subsystems.

For example, the `google docs` subsystem is mounted to a main server using the following bean definition in the `bootstrap-context.xml` (`<install_folder>\tomcat\webapps\alfresco\WEB-INF\classes\alfresco`) file. The ID of the bean is the category of the subsystem:

```
<bean id=""googledocs"" class=""org.alfresco.repo.management.
subsystems.ChildApplicationContextFactory"" parent=""abstractProperty
BackedBean"">
<property name=""autoStart"">
<value>true</value>
</property>
</bean>
```

You can have a folder with a name as the category within different subsystems, such as `<install_folder>\tomcat\webapps\alfresco\WEB-INF\classes\alfresco\subsystem\googledocs`

Extending the subsystem

To extend the subsystem, you can follow these steps as per your requirements:

- For the configuration of any subsystem properties, add your changes in the `alfresco-global.properties` file at `<install_folder>\tomcat\shared\classes`, or this can be done via JMX as well, which you will learn more about in *Chapter 9, Maintenance and Troubleshooting*. After making changes in the `alfresco-global.properties` file, restart Alfresco.
- In case you need a separate properties file for each subsystem, place your properties file at `<extension>/subsystems/<category>/<type>/<id>/*.properties`

- Let's take an example of a Fileserver subsystem. It doesn't have multiple implementations, so the type and ID of such a system is default. We place our files at extension>/subsystems/fileServers/default/default/custom-fileserver.properties.
- To extend any configuration, create a custom context file and place it at <extension>/subsystems/<category>/<type>/<id>/*-context.xml.
- For a Fileserver subsystem, any configuration of beans would go into <extension>/subsystems/fileServers/default/default/custom-fileserver-context.xml.

Repository configuration

There are different components in Alfresco, such as a database, e-mail, search, audit, and so on, each with its own configuration properties. The following section covers details about all of these configurations.

> Note that changes to these configurations would require a restart of the Alfresco server.

Configuring the database

A database is one of the key attributes of Alfresco. It is generally configured at the time of installation. Along with DB connection parameters, there are some tuning parameters for database connection pooling. These parameters are based on a repository's read/write operation. Alfresco supports multiple databases such as MySQL, PostgreSQL, Oracle, and so on. Configuring a proper connection for a URL allows for connection to the supported database.

Here are some important database properties. Add and modify the values of these properties in the alfresco-global.properties file. Default settings are present in the repository.properties file:

- db.name: The name of the database; by default, it is alfresco
- db.driver: The full, qualified name of the JDBC driver class; for the PostgreSQL database, it is org.postgresql.Driver.
- db.url: The JDBC connection URL, for example, for a PostgreSQL connection, it is jdbc:postgresql://localhost:5445/${db.name}.
- db.username: The username to connect to a database.
- db.password: The password to connect to a database.

- `db.pool.initial`: The number of connections to be kept open when the DB connection pool is initialized.
- `db.pool.max`: The maximum number of connections that can be opened in the DB connection pool; this is an important property to configure depending on the type of database. It's value should be less than the max value set for the database connection that's supported.
- `db.pool.validate.query`: The SQL query to validate whether a connection is still alive. The value of this property changes based on the database type. This property is useful to use along with other flags when `testOnBorrow`, `testonreturn` is enabled. Here are the properties that control this flag:
    - `db.pool.validate.borrow=true`
    - `db.pool.validate.return=false`

Here are the properties related to evicting or abandoning a connection from the connection pool:

- `db.pool.evict.interval`: The sleep interval in milliseconds between each eviction process. By default, it is set to `-1`, which means disabled.
- `db.pool.evict.idle.min`: The idle time in milliseconds before a connection can be evicted.
- `db.pool.evict.validate`: The flag required to validate a connection before eviction.
- `db.pool.abandoned.detect`: The flag required to enable or disable the detection of an abandoned connection.
- `db.pool.abandoned.time`: Time taken in milliseconds for an abandoned connection to become eligible for removal.
- `db.pool.abandoned.log`: The flag required to log an abandoned connection. If enabled, it will print in a log file when any abandoned connection is removed.

Refer to `http://commons.apache.org/proper/commons-dbcp/configuration.html` for more details about database connection pool configurations.

Configuring the content store

The content store in Alfresco is a filesystem location where binary files are stored. Configuring it is very easy, but this should be done only at time of installation.

Add and modify the following properties in `alfresco-global.properties` to configure the content store:

```
dir.root=/mnt/data/alf_data<Specify the path of the Root directory
where contentstore would be created. Make sure it is always absolute
path>

dir.contentstore=${dir.root}/contentstore<Contenstore specific path.
dir.contentstore.deleted=${dir.root}/contentstore.deleted<File
location for deleted contentstore. Files purged from Alfresco system
are stored in this directory.  You can specify a different path if you
want to keep this directory in different location.>
```

Alfresco also allows multiple content stores, and you can store documents in the selected content store. More details about this are covered in *Chapter 8, The Basics of the Alfresco Content Store*.

Configuring the search functionality

Alfresco 5.x supports only one search engine, `Solr`. Older versions of Alfresco used to also support Lucene, which is now deprecated. `Solr` can be installed as embedded within the Alfresco installation, or it can be installed on a separate instance.

Here are the three properties that you can add and modify in `alfresco-global.properties`:

```
index.subsystem.name=solr4<Defines the search subsystem you want.
Values could be either solr4, solr, or none.>

dir.keystore=${dir.root}/keystore<This is the path of the certificate
keystore as alfresco and solr uses https connection to communicate.>

solr.port.ssl=8443 : <Solrapplication SSL port>
```

Further details on how to switch between different search subsystems, and configuring and tuning `Solr` will be covered in *Chapter 5, Search*.

Configuring Google Docs

Google Docs is one of the subsystems in Alfresco. It allows users to edit documents stored in Alfresco using Google Docs. Documents in Alfresco are checked out in Google Docs and once edited, they are checked-in to Alfresco. There will be only a single Google account used by all, so make sure you create a Google account that can be configured in Alfresco.

Add and modify the following properties in the `alfresco-global.properties` file from `<TOMCAT_HOME>/webapps/alfresco/WEB-INF/classes/alfresco/subsystems/googledocs/default/googledocs.properties` and configure it as per your needs:

```
googledocs.googleeditable.enabled=true<Flag to enable/disable the
Google docs>

googledocs.username <Google account username>

googledocs.password <Google account password>
```

You can also configure Google Docs using the mechanism that extends any subsystem, as explained in the *Configuring Subsystem in Alfresco* section.

Auditing

Alfresco captures certain actions taken by a user on any node in the repository via an audit mechanism. Using audit, trail administrators can identify which user viewed, created, copied, or deleted content in the repository. Let's look at an example where the Alfresco repository is being used to manage all the contracts of an organization. It becomes critical to maintain a history of all the actions taken by users in the system on these contracts from a security perspective. So, Alfresco should be configured to enable this audit and the kind of data that needs to be audited.

Auditing in Alfresco can be easily configured based on requirements. You can control the amount of data that you want to audit.

Here are the default settings from `repository.properites` located at `<TOMCAT_HOME>/webapps/alfresco/WEB-INF/classes/alfresco`. To configure audit properties, add and modify the required properties in `alfresco-global.properties`:

```
audit.enabled=true < Flag to enable or disable the audit>

audit.alfresco-access.enabled=false<Configure it to enable the
audit alfresco-access application. This is alfresco default audit
application. This property need to be enabled which enables data
capture for audit>

audit.dod5015.enabled=false <This flag is for enabling audit for
records management module>

audit.filter.alfresco-access.default.enabled=true
```

```
audit.filter.alfresco-access.transaction.user=~System;~null;.*
<This filters determines the user for whom you want to capture the
audit. Current default configuration audits all users activity except
System user>

audit.filter.alfresco-access.transaction.type=cm:folder;cm:conte
nt;st:site<This filter allows you to control the type of data to
audit. If you have custom type defined like org:contract for contract
documents, you can add those to capture audit for only certain types
of documents>

audit.filter.alfresco-
access.transaction.path=~/sys:archivedItem;~/ver:;.*<Filters out the
path of the transaction. Default configuration audits anything except
archived item>
```

You can change these filters as per your business needs to audit only certain amounts of data.

Configuring file servers

The document stored in Alfresco can be accessed via a filesystem using CIFS/FTP with the File Servers subsystem, which is one of the unique qualities of Alfresco. Alfresco authenticated users can only retrieve documents using this protocol.

The File servers subsystem can be configured via `alfresco-global.properties` or JMX. To configure XML files, use a standard extension mechanism for the subsystem.

The following are some generic filesystem properties you might need to change based on your system needs.

Modify this property value if the name of the filesystem needs to be changed:

```
filesystem.name=Alfresco
```

Modify the following property value if the root directory where the filesystem should open needs to be changed:

```
filesystem.storeName=${spaces.store}
filesystem.rootPath=${protocols.rootPath}
```

Configuring CIFS

The SMB/CIFS protocol is implemented based on a Java socket code, which leverages Alfresco to use CIFS on any platform. The default settings use the JNI-based implementation for Windows and a Java socket for Linux and other platforms.

Now, to configure CIFS based on your network and requirements, you need to add and modify these properties in the `alfresco-global.properties` file. The default settings are in <TOMCAT_HOME>/webapps/alfresco/WEB-INF/classes/alfresco/subsystems/fileServers/default/file-servers.properties:

- `cifs.enabled`: This property enables or disables CIFS
- `cifs.serverName`: This should be a unique 16-character server name. If you have multiple instances of Alfresco on the same machine, you need to have different names. The default value is `${localname}A`.
- `cifs.domain`: If a value is specified, it shows the domain/workgroup that the server belongs to. By default, it takes the domain of the server.
- `cifs.broadcast`: This specifies a broadcast mask for a network.
- `cifs.bindto`: This is mainly required if you want to use CIFS on a Unix-based platform. Specify the network adapter that it should be bound to. By default, it is bound to all adapters.
- `cifs.hostannounce`: This is a flag that allows the CIFS server to be announced in a local domain or workgroup.
- `cifs.disableNativeCode`: This property will only be effected on Windows. It allows you to disable the use of a native JNI-based CIFS implementation. If you deactivate JNI, you need to make some changes to the Windows configuration for CIFS to work with a default Java socket-based implementation.
- `cifs.sessionTimeout`: The CIFS session timeout value in seconds. If no I/O operation occurs within this specified interval, the server will terminate the session. You can increase it as per the standard across all systems.

The following four properties are useful when you have your Alfresco server on a Unix-based platform. CIFS needs access to privileged ports; for that, Alfresco should be started as the root user. If this is not the case, then you have to configure these properties for non-privileged ports. Set firewall rules to route the request from privileged ports to non-privileged ones. There are a few firewall examples at `http://docs.alfresco.com/5.0/tasks/fileserv-CIFS-useracc.html` for reference.

```
cifs.tcpipSMB.port=445
cifs.netBIOSSMB.sessionPort=139
cifs.netBIOSSMB.namePort=137
cifs.netBIOSSMB.datagramPort=138
```

Configuring FTP

Alfresco also supports the FTP protocol for accessing content. To configure FTP, either change the configuration in `alfresco-global.properties` or JMX. Alfresco also supports secure FTPS.

To configure FTP, add and modify the following properties in the `alfresco-global.properties` file from `<TOMCAT_HOME>/webapps/alfresco/WEB-INF/classes/alfresco/subsystems/fileServers/default/file-servers.properties`. Keep only the properties you want to configure; the unchanged one will be referred to from the default settings.

```
ftp.enabled=true<Configure to enable or disable FTP server>

ftp.port=21<Port on which FTP server is listening for connection. Make
sure this port is open.>

ftp.bindto  < Specify the network adapter server should bound to. By
default if kept blank it would bind to all network adapters>
```

Let's look at the settings for a secure FTP connection. All these settings are required to enable FTPS. You need to specify the path, the passphrase for `keyStore` and `trustStore`, and the type.

```
ftp.keyStore
ftp.keyStoreType
ftp.keyStorePassphrase
ftp.trustStore
ftp.trustStoreType
ftp.trustStorePassphrase
```

The following setting will force all sessions to be secured:

```
ftp.requireSecureSession=true
```

For more details, you can refer to the Alfresco wiki at `https://wiki.alfresco.com/wiki/File_Server_Subsystem_4.0`.

Configuring the cloud sync service

Alfresco supports the hybrid model, which allows the synchronizing of content between the on-premise setup to the Alfresco cloud. Selected documents can be shared on the cloud for a broader audience to access. For enabling cloud sync, you need to have Alfresco Enterprise and the Enterprise license with the Sync feature enabled. Install your enterprise license and restart Alfresco server. The **Sync to Cloud** action in Share will allow you to share the document on the cloud.

Alfresco doesn't support multiple identical instances of on-premise Enterprise Alfresco to sync with the cloud. So, on the other instances, you need to disable sync by setting the following property in `alfresco-global.properties`:

```
syncService.mode=OFF
sync.pushJob.enabled=false
sync.pullJob.enabled=false
```

Also, the server mode should be set to production on the main production server for the hybrid sync cloud to work, as follows:

```
system.serverMode=PRODUCTION<On other server you can set value as TEST or BACKUP>
```

Configuring e-mail

E-mail is one of the subsystems of Alfresco and supports both inbound and outbound e-mails. Using the inbound e-mail subsystem, Alfresco can be used to manage e-mails. E-mails can be stored in Alfresco like normal content, with the e-mail body and attachments.

Outbound e-mail configuration

To configure the outbound e-mail subsystem , add and modify these properties in `alfresco-global.properties`. The default settings are in `<TOMCAT_HOME>/webapps/alfresco/WEB-INF/classes/alfresco/subsystems\email\OutboundSMTP`.

```
mail.host= <Configure SMTP server of your network>
mail.port=<Proper SMTP port. Default port is 25>

<If authentication required then provide proper username and password>
mail.username=
mail.password =

mail.from.default=<Set proper default from email address. While
sending email from Alfresco from address is not present this default
value would be taken>
```

Alfresco also supports SMTPS; these properties need to be changed to enable it:

```
mail.smtps.auth=false
mail.smtps.starttls.enable=false
```

Inbound e-mail configuration

In order to configure Alfresco as an inbound e-mail server, add the following property to the `alfresco-global.properties` file and configure it as required. You can remove any unmodified values. The default settings are present in the `<TOMCAT_HOME>/webapps/alfresco/WEB-INF/classes/subsystems/email/InboundSMTP/inboundSMTP.properties` file.

```
email.server.port= provide port of your email server(default 25)
email.server.domain= provide domain address of your email server
email.inbound.emailContributorsAuthority = group name that user
should be member of to be able to add email. Default value is EMAIL_
CONTRIBUTORS
```

Also, there are other settings in the file, such as blocked list and allowed list, which can be configured as per your requirements.

IMAP configuration

Alfresco also supports connecting to a repository using the IMAP protocol. Users can use IMAP e-mail clients such as Outlook and Thunderbird to connect to Alfresco. Users can just drag and drop e-mails to the Alfresco repository.

To configure IMAP, add and modify the following properties in `alfresco-global.properties` as per your requirements. The default settings are present in `<TOMCAT_HOME> /webapps/alfresco/WEB-INF/classes/alfresco/subsystems/imap/default/imap-server.properties`.

```
imap.server.enabled= <Set true to enable the IMAP. By default it is
disabled>
imap.server.host=x.x.x.x < Set server host address>
imap.server.folder.cache.size=10000 <Change this value if there are
large number of folders. Increasing this value would have an impact on
memory>

imap.mail.from.default=<Set proper default from email address>
imap.mail.to.default=<Set proper default to email address>

<Change this values if you want to change the rootimap folder path>
imap.config.home.store=${protocols.storeName}
imap.config.home.rootPath=${protocols.rootPath}
imap.config.home.folderPath=Imap Home

imap.server.port=143<Configure proper IMAP server port. And make sure
this port is open on server>
```

Alfresco also support IMAPS. Configure below property to enable it. Keystore used by IMAPS should be defined in Java System properties.

```
imap.server.imaps.enabled=false
imap.server.imaps.port=993
```

Summary

Alfresco provides highly extensible architecture. It is easy to configure and extend the system. Alfresco provides an extension file, `alfresco-global.properties`, which is used to modify any configuration properties. There are extension directories, where the configuration XML files are placed to extend it.

Important components in Alfresco are embedded as different subsystems. Subsystems can also be extended by changing property files or via JMX.

In this chapter, we also learned about the important properties and files for the entire subsystem and repository configuration.

The next chapter will cover details about administration in Alfresco and Share. It will cover details about the Alfresco admin console and the workflow console.

4
Administration of Alfresco

For any Enterprise-level software, administration of your system is critical. Alfresco provides a simple and user-friendly interface to administrate and configure various important services. Users and groups can be very efficiently managed by admin users.

This chapter provides you with an introduction on ways to administer Alfresco.

By the end of this chapter, you will have learned about:

- Understanding Alfresco Explorer and the Share admin console
- Groups and user creation
- Administration of workflow
- How to use Node Browser

Understanding the admin console

Alfresco provide three types of administration console:

- Alfresco standalone administration page.
- Admin console in Alfresco Share.
- Admin console in Alfresco Explorer. This Explorer is being completely deprecated in Alfresco version 5.0, as some features are being made available in Share now.

Alfresco standalone administration page

This is a standalone administration console in Alfresco, which allows you to configure and manage the Alfresco repository. This console is available only in the Enterprise version and is restricted to admin users. This interface is external to Alfresco Explorer and Share.

Use the following URL to access the admin console. It will prompt for user credentials. Provide admin user credentials to access it:

- http://<IP>:<Port>/alfresco/service/enterprise/admin

The landing page is the summary of all the configurations. There are various configurations available in this console. Let's go through each of them in detail.

System summary

This is the landing page for the admin console. It provides details about all the configurations of the repository such as JDK version, Alfresco path, file server, e-mail configuration, auditing, content-store location, indexes, and users and groups in the system.

The following snapshot shows the configuration details in the summary section. **System Information** shows details about the server. The **Indexing Subsystem** section shows which type of subsystem is enabled for searches. The **Content Stores** section shows the path and size of contentstore.

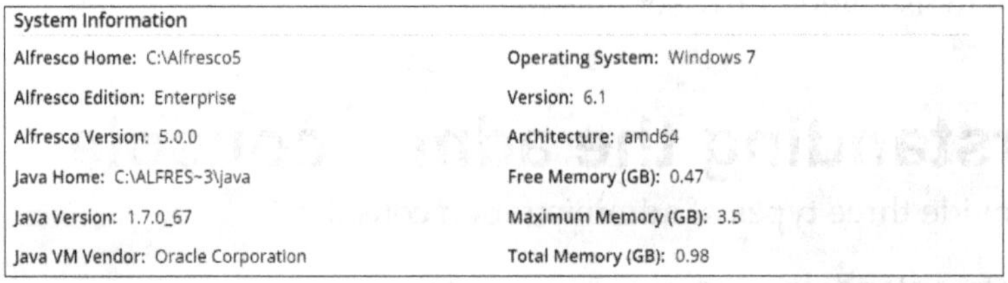
System Information
Alfresco Home: C:\Alfresco5
Operating System: Windows 7
Alfresco Edition: Enterprise
Version: 6.1
Alfresco Version: 5.0.0
Architecture: amd64
Java Home: C:\ALFRES~3\java
Free Memory (GB): 0.47
Java Version: 1.7.0_67
Maximum Memory (GB): 3.5
Java VM Vendor: Oracle Corporation
Total Memory (GB): 0.98

Transformation Services
Office Suite: Disabled
JOD Converter: Enabled
SWF Tools: Enabled
ImageMagic: Enabled
FFMpeg: Not Installed
Indexing Subsystem
Solr: Disabled
Solr 4: Enabled
No Index: Disabled
Alfresco Access: Disabled
Tagging: Enabled
Sync: Enabled
Content Stores
Store Path: C:\Alfresco5\alf_data\contentstore
Space Used (MB): 255,373
Space Available (MB): 220,776
Store Path: C:\Alfresco5\alf_data\contentstore.deleted
Space Used (MB): 255,373
Space Available (MB): 220,776
Store Path: C:\Alfresco5\tomcat\temp\Alfresco
Space Used (MB): 255,373
Space Available (MB): 220,776

Consoles

The console section provides an interface to execute the commands to load the message bundle, model files, and perform an operation on workflows. This section is divided into three categories:

- Model and messages console
- Tenant console
- Workflow console

Model and messages console

This console allows you to manage the models and message bundles. Alfresco allows you to define custom content type and its schema in `.xml` configuration files, which are called model files. Place the file in the extension directory and you can load the changes into Alfresco. You can activate or deactivate the content model via command execution:

1. Type `help` to get a list of all the commands.

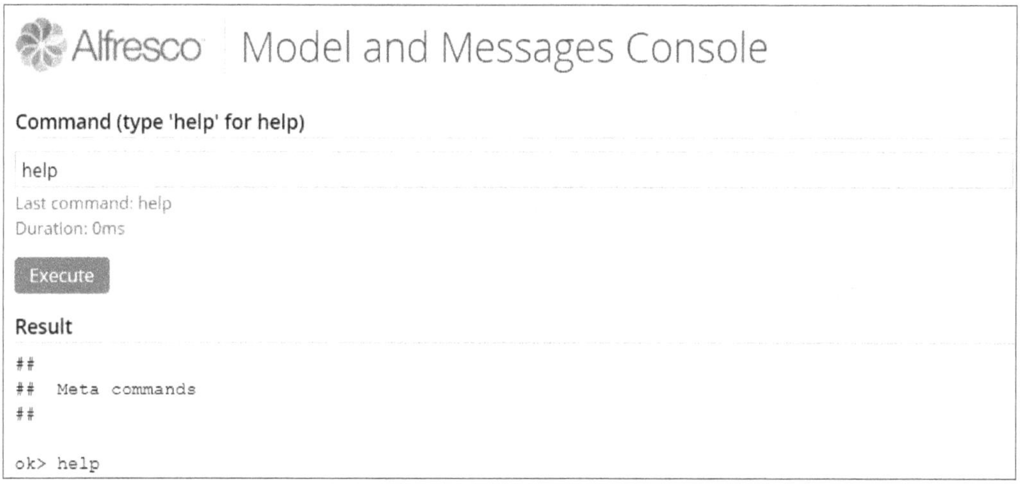
Alfresco
Model and Messages Console
Command (type 'help' for help)
help
Last command: help
Duration: 0ms
Execute
Result
##
Meta commands
##
ok> help

2. For example, let's say the marketing team is your Alfresco repository, and you need to categorize a brochures type of content so it can be filtered out easily and you also require additional metadata such as published date and who authorized the content. Here, we need to define a new custom content type in the custom model file and deploy it in Alfresco. The following steps are required to create a new content type named `brochure`.

3. Create `customModel.xml`. Here is a snippet of the code. A new content type named `brochure` is created:

   ```
   ...
   <types>
     <type name="custom:brochure">
       <title>Brochures</title>
       <parent>cm:content</parent>
         <properties>
           <property name="custom:publishedDate">
           <type>d:datetime</type>
       </property>
       <property name="custom:authorisedBy">
   <type>d:text</type>
   </property>
   </properties>
   </type>
   </types>
   ..
   ```

4. Place this file in the Alfresco installation directory (`<Alfresco_Home>/tomcat/shared/classes/alfresco/extension`).
5. Execute the following command in the model and messages console, this would deploy the model and activate it:

   ```
   deploy model alfresco/extension/customModel.xml
   ```

6. By default, the deployment model gets activated, if you want to deactivate the model execute the following command:

   ```
   deactivate model customModel.xml
   ```

In a similar way you can deploy and undeploy the message bundle.

> Model files can be undeployed only if they are not used by any content.
>
> In versions prior to Alfresco 5.0, this same feature is available as a repo admin console (`http://<IP>:<Port>/alfresco/faces/jsp/admin/repoadmin-console.jsp`).

Tenant console

The tenant console allows you to administrate and manage the different tenants in Alfresco. Alfresco supports multitenancy where a single instance of Alfresco can be divided into different tenants. Each tenant is a logical partition representing an independent instance of Alfresco. For end users it appears they are accessing separate instances of Alfresco. Each tenant will have its own set of users, folders, and content. Using this tenant console you can create, delete, enable, and disable tenants. It also allows you to import and export content from tenants.

For example, if each department in your organization needs their content and users completely separated, creating a different tenant for each department is one of the ways to achieve this with a single instance of Alfresco.

To create a new tenant, execute the following command. This will create a tenant named `digitalmarketing.com` and the admin user for this tenant will be `joe1234`. Each tenant can have a different admin user:

```
create digitalmarketing.com joe1234
```

Execute the help command to see a list of all the available commands.

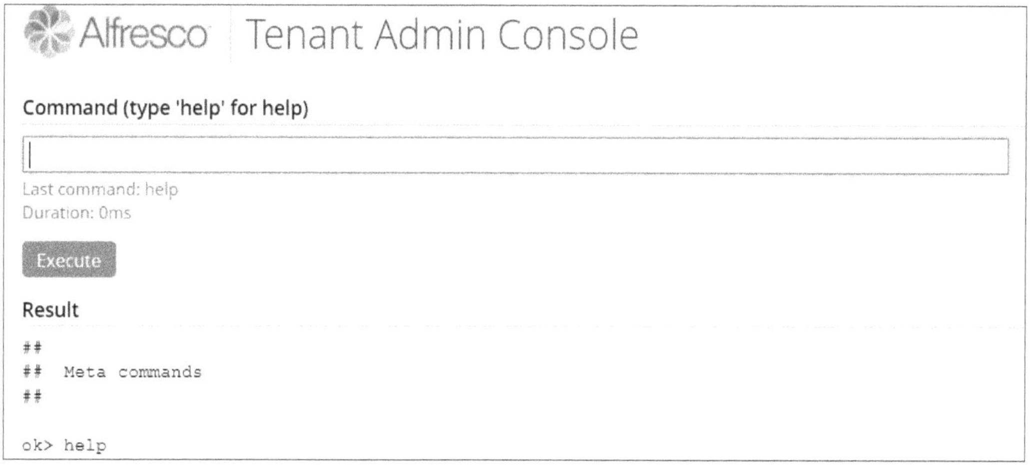
Alfresco
Tenant Admin Console
Command (type 'help' for help)
Last command: help
Duration: 0ms
Execute
Result
##
Meta commands
##
ok> help

In the version prior to Alfresco 5.0 this feature is available by using the following URL:

- http://<IP>:<Port>/alfresco/faces/jsp/admin/tenantadmin-console.jsp

Workflow console

This console allows you to manage and administer workflows using various commands. You can deploy and undeploy workflows from the repository. Using this console you can query the task details of any process in the workflow, start a workflow, and other tasks.

Important commands from an administrator standpoint:

- To get a list of all the workflows that are completed or are in an in-flight state, they can be retrieved using the following command. This command takes time to execute when there are a large number of workflows:

  ```
  show workflows all
  ```

- If you want to get a list of workflows of specific definitions, you can use the following list of commands. For example, let's say we want to find the list of all Review Approve workflows:

  1. First, fetch the workflow definition list using the following command:

     ```
     show definitions all
     ```

  2. Set the definition ID in the console to execute a further command. Here, we are taking an example of the Review Approve workflow, which has an ID as `activiti$activitiReview:1:8`

     ```
     use definition activiti$activitiReview:1:8
     ```

  3. Now, execute the following command to fetch all the workflows for this definition. The result of this command will provide the workflow ID, description, start date, and definition name. The structure of any workflow ID is `activiti$<Numeric ID>`.

     ```
     show workflows.
     ```

     The output obtained is shown here:

     ```
     id: activiti$101 , desc: review the details and provide
     comments , start date: Sun Jan 11 18:41:07 PST 2015 , def:
     activiti$activitiReview
     ```

  4. You can also get into more granular details such as task details of any workflow instance, as each workflow would have different stages. For example, for the workflow `activiti$101`, we want to get the task details, so we need to execute the following set of commands:

     ```
     use workflow activiti$101
     show tasks
     ```

The output obtained is shown here:

```
task id: activiti$145 , name: wf:activitiReviewTask ,
properties: 19
```

- This console is also useful to delete any specific in-flight workflows, all workflows from the repository, and specific tasks of the workflow. For example, we want to delete the workflow with the ID `activiti$101`, so we need to execute the following command:

```
delete workflow activiti$101
```

- To delete all workflows from the repository, execute the following command. Be very cautious when using this command:

```
delete all workflows
```

> If you have a large number of workflows in the repository, this command will slow down your system and may take a large amount of time to execute.

In the version prior to Alfresco 5.0, this feature is available using the following URL: `http://<IP>:<port>/alfresco/faces/jsp/admin/workflow-console.jsp`.

E-mail services

Alfresco provides two kinds of e-mail services: inbound and outbound e-mails.

Inbound e-mail services allows users to store their e-mails in Alfresco as content along with attachments. Alfresco becomes a repository for e-mail storage. This **Inbound Email** admin page allows you to enable or disable services and configure them as per requirements. The following screenshot shows details about the configuration:

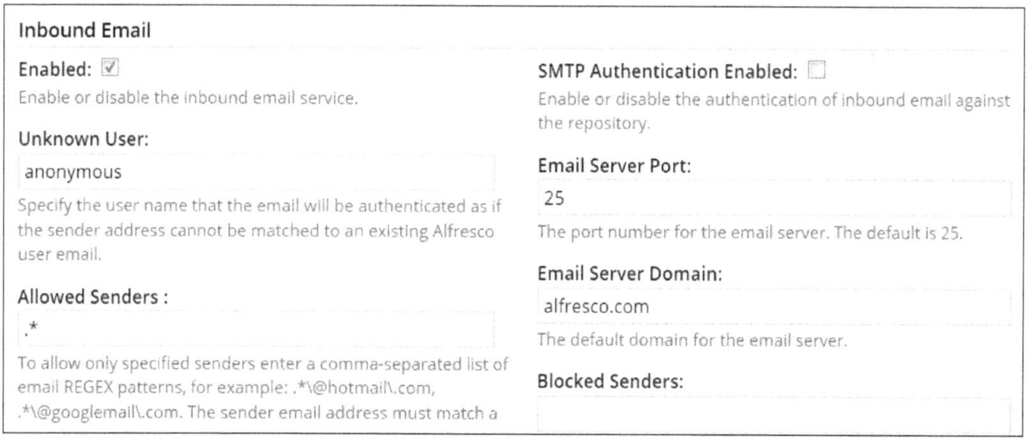

Inbound Email
Enabled:
Enable or disable the inbound email service.
Unknown User:
anonymous
Specify the user name that the email will be authenticated as if the sender address cannot be matched to an existing Alfresco user email.
Allowed Senders :
.*
To allow only specified senders enter a comma-separated list of email REGEX patterns, for example: .*\@hotmail\.com, .*\@googlemail\.com. The sender email address must match a
SMTP Authentication Enabled:
Enable or disable the authentication of inbound email against the repository.
Email Server Port:
25
The port number for the email server. The default is 25.
Email Server Domain:
alfresco.com
The default domain for the email server.
Blocked Senders:

Outbound e-mails control all e-mails sent to users from the Alfresco repository. This page allows you to configure and manage the SMTP server details. It also has a **Test Email** section, which you can use to confirm whether the configurations are correct and e-mails are being sent. The following screenshot shows details about the configuration available:

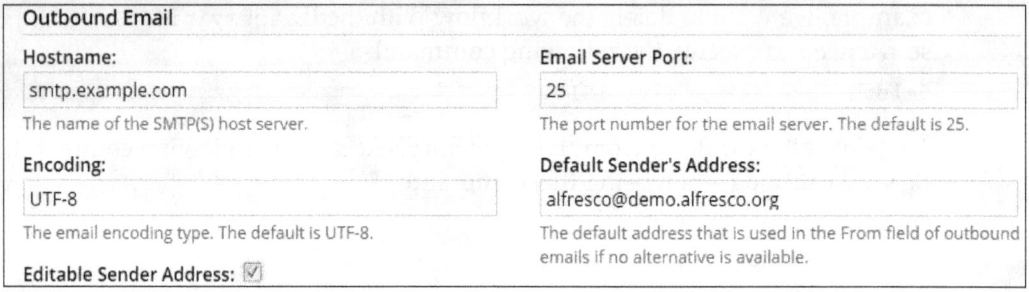
Outbound Email
Hostname:
smtp.example.com
The name of the SMTP(S) host server.
Email Server Port:
25
The port number for the email server. The default is 25.
Encoding:
UTF-8
The email encoding type. The default is UTF-8.
Default Sender's Address:
alfresco@demo.alfresco.org
The default address that is used in the From field of outbound emails if no alternative is available.
Editable Sender Address:

As shown in the following screenshot, you can also send a test message to confirm the configurations are working properly:

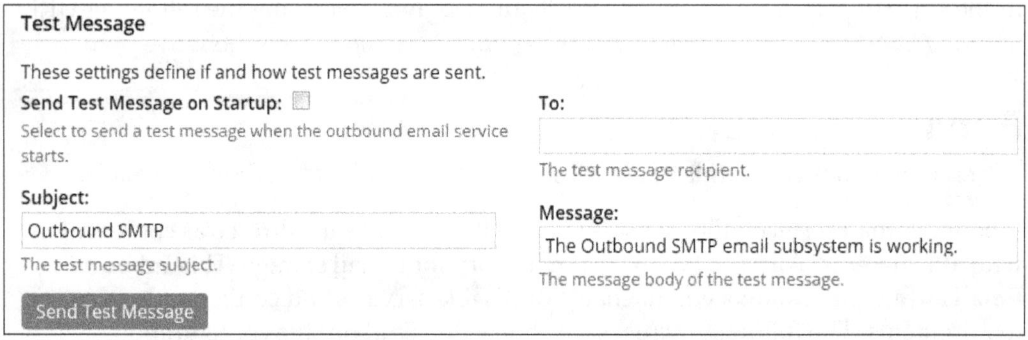
Test Message
These settings define if and how test messages are sent.
Send Test Message on Startup:
Select to send a test message when the outbound email service starts.
Subject:
Outbound SMTP
The test message subject.
Send Test Message
To:
The test message recipient.
Message:
The Outbound SMTP email subsystem is working.
The message body of the test message.

The configurations are the same as we learnt in *Chapter 3, Alfresco Configuration*. With the admin console you can configure the service at runtime without restarting Alfresco.

General

In this section, we will discuss the following topics:

- License
- Repository information
- System settings

License

The Enterprise Edition of Alfresco needs a license for installation. This admin page allows you to manage the license file. The license is not bound to the server, but it restricts the number of users, amount of content, and type of support from Alfresco.

This page provides details such as valid date of license, usage information, clustering support, content-store encryption, and cloud sync. By default, Alfresco provides a 30-day trial license as shown in the following screenshot:

License: Enterprise - v5.0
Licensed Alfresco version.
License Type: ENTERPRISE
Type of license issued.
Issued: Dec 22, 2014 11:23:06 PM
Date license was issued by Alfresco.
License Holder: O=Trial User
Name of license holder. This should be your company name.
Days: 30
Number of days that your license covers.
Issuer: CN=Unknown, OU=Unknown, O=Alfresco, L=Maidenhead, ST=Berkshire, C=UK
Original location where the license was generated.

The license file received from Alfresco has the extension `.lic`. You can upload the license file to the Alfresco repository or copy it in the Alfresco installation path and apply the license file as shown in the following screenshot. Once the license file is installed successfully, the file extension will be changed to `<license-name>.lic.installed`.

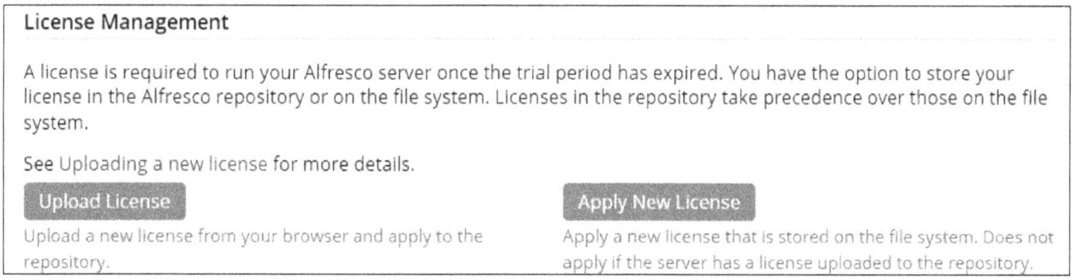
License Management
A license is required to run your Alfresco server once the trial period has expired. You have the option to store your license in the Alfresco repository or on the file system. Licenses in the repository take precedence over those on the file system.
See Uploading a new license for more details.
Upload License
Upload a new license from your browser and apply to the repository.
Apply New License
Apply a new license that is stored on the file system. Does not apply if the server has a license uploaded to the repository.

> If there are new features enabled with the new license, an Alfresco server restart is required.

Repository information

This section provides details about the repository such as unique ID, which is important when communicating with the server using the CMIS protocol. It also provides the version and build details of Alfresco. These details are required when you need support from Alfresco or you are upgrading the repository.

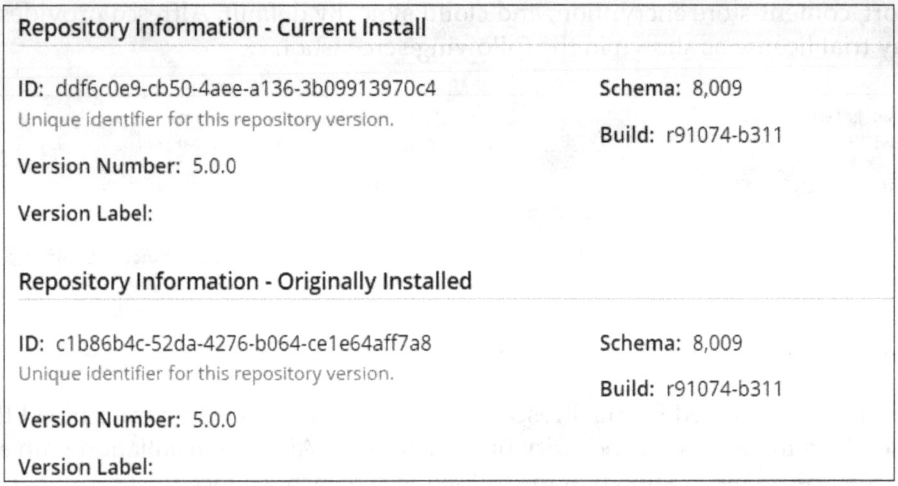
Repository Information - Current Install
ID: ddf6c0e9-cb50-4aee-a136-3b09913970c4
Unique identifier for this repository version.
Schema: 8,009
Build: r91074-b311
Version Number: 5.0.0
Version Label:
Repository Information - Originally Installed
ID: c1b86b4c-52da-4276-b064-ce1e64aff7a8
Unique identifier for this repository version.
Schema: 8,009
Build: r91074-b311
Version Number: 5.0.0
Version Label:

System settings

These settings are for the repository and Share application configurations. There are three sections: **Alfresco Repository Settings**, **Server Settings**, and **Share Application Settings**:

- **Alfresco Repository Settings** shows the details about the repository port, IP address, and protocol that can be used to communicate with the server. This page does not allow you to change values, you can configure these values in the `alfresco-global.properties` file.
- **Server Settings** allows you to configure the maximum number of users who can use the system. You can also control the users who can only log in to the system by configuring the user list in **Allowed Users**. If the admin user who is setting this allowed users list does not enter their name in the list, the system will automatically take that username in allowed users, and this current user would not be locked out of the system. The username list in the allowed users configuration should match with the username in the Alfresco repository.

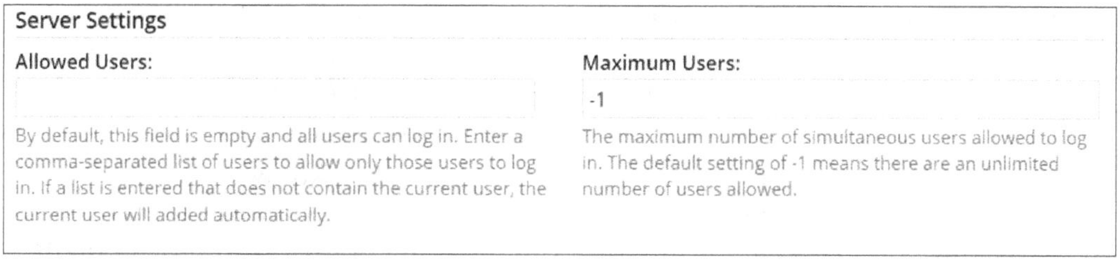
Server Settings
Allowed Users:
By default, this field is empty and all users can log in. Enter a comma-separated list of users to allow only those users to log in. If a list is entered that does not contain the current user, the current user will added automatically.
Maximum Users:
-1
The maximum number of simultaneous users allowed to log in. The default setting of -1 means there are an unlimited number of users allowed.

- **Share Application Settings** section allows you to configure the IP address, port, and protocol to access the Share application. As the Share application can be installed independent to Alfresco, we can change the configuration of the repository to point to a different Share instance. You can also configure the group details who have access to all the public sites in Share.

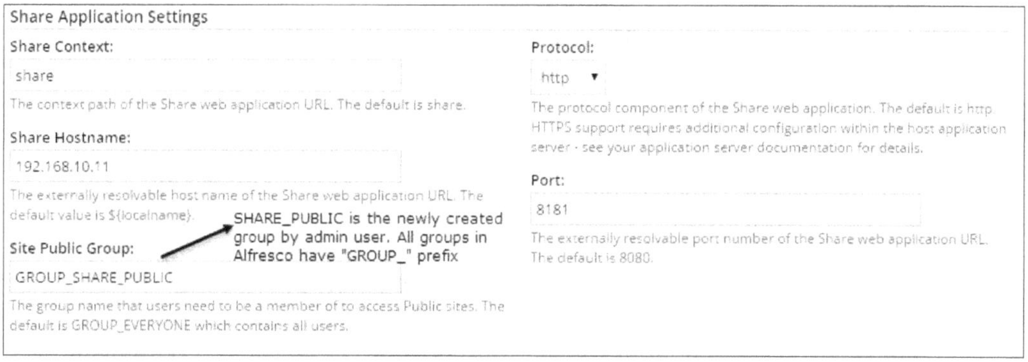
Share Application Settings
Share Context:
share
The context path of the Share web application URL. The default is share.
Share Hostname:
192.168.10.11
The externally resolvable host name of the Share web application URL. The default value is ${localname}.
SHARE_PUBLIC is the newly created group by admin user. All groups in Alfresco have "GROUP_" prefix
Site Public Group:
GROUP_SHARE_PUBLIC
The group name that users need to be a member of to access Public sites. The default is GROUP_EVERYONE which contains all users.
Protocol:
http
The protocol component of the Share web application. The default is http. HTTPS support requires additional configuration within the host application server - see your application server documentation for details.
Port:
8181
The externally resolvable port number of the Share web application URL. The default is 8080.

Repository services

This section of the admin page allows you to configure various core services of the Alfresco repository such as search, activity feed, replication, and so on.

Let's see details about each of the service configurations:

- **Activities Feed**: When enabled, this service allows all users in the Alfresco repository to receive e-mails about their activities and the activity of the people they are following. These feeds are the same as the **My Activity** dashlet in Share. If enabled, you can configure the frequency of the feed to be sent to users. The time duration of activities, such as only activities of the past 10 days, should be sent in feeds and also control the number of activities. Enable this service only when required and remember to time the feed scheduler for when there is much less usage of the repository. By default, this service should always be kept disabled as it will create an unnecessary load on the system.

- **Repository Server Clustering**: This page just shows the details about the clustering enabled/disabled and Cluster ID. More information about clustering will be covered in *Chapter 7, High Availability in Alfresco.*
- **Process Engines**: Alfresco supports two workflow engines: Activiti and jBPM. In this section you can enable/disable the workflow engine you need. By default, Activiti is enabled and it is recommended to use this engine only. This page also shows you the count of total workflow in-flight and total tasks.
- **Replication Service**: One of the nice features in Alfresco is that it allows you to replicate the content from one repository to another by defining replication jobs. These jobs contain details about the target server, folders to be copied, and timing of when this should be triggered. These jobs are controlled by the Replication Service. You have to enable the Replication Service using the setting **Replication Enabled**, before you can define your jobs to replicate content. This section also allows you to define the permission of the replicated content on the target repository, if **Read Only Replication** is enabled, all content in the target repository would be Read Only.
- **Search Service**: Search Service is the backbone of the search in Alfresco. Search Service talks to search engines such as Solr and Lucene. By default, the Solr4 search engine is used since Alfresco v 5.0. This section allows administrators to configure and manage search servers by configuring the IP address, port, HTTP, and so on. You can also configure the backup location and timings for Solr indexes. If Solr is embedded in Alfresco there is no change required in default configurations. More details about search engines and their monitoring will be covered in *Chapter 5, Search*.
- **Subscription Service**: In Alfresco Share, there is a functionality where a user can follow other users in the repository and they can view activities about other users. This is controlled by the Subscription Service. You have to enable the Subscription Service if you want to allow users to follow each other and view other users' activities. By default, this feature is enabled.
- **Transformation Service**: Alfresco supports transformation of content in various file formats such as Word documents to PDF, image `.jpeg` to `.png`, `.pdf` to `.swf`, and so on. These transformations are controlled by various transformation services, which internally use various tools such as Openoffice, ImageMagick, and SWF tools. This page allows you to control and manage these transformation tools. It is recommended not to change the default settings unless it is required.

Support tools

These are some additional tools that help administrators get details about the repository and help them in troubleshooting:

- **Node Browser**: This browser allows the administrator user to navigate through the complete repository and view details about all nodes such as folders, rules, users, system folders, and so on. Node Browser is a very useful and important tool from an administration standpoint. More details are covered in a later part of this chapter.
- **Download JMX Dump**: You can download the complete configuration and system details of the Alfresco repository in a `.zip` file as shown in the following screenshot. This file is very useful to the person troubleshooting the system.

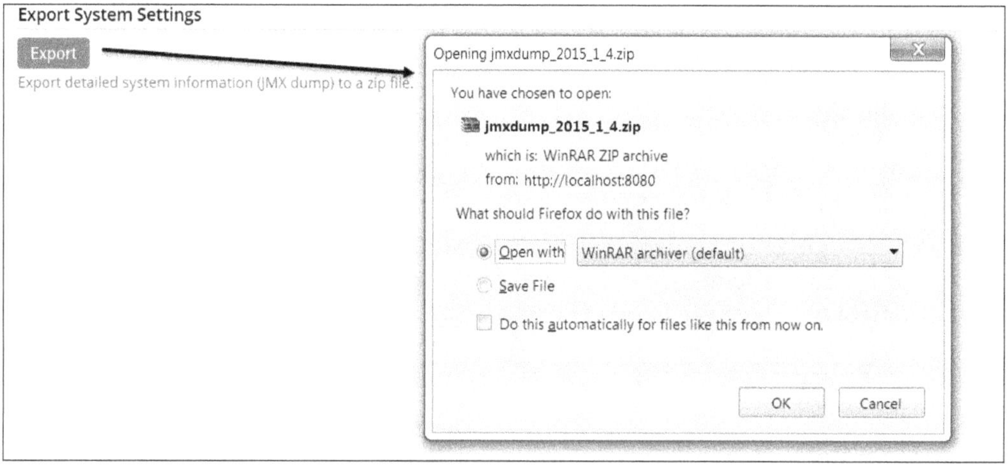
Export System Settings
Export
Export detailed system information (JMX dump) to a zip file.
Opening jmxdump_2015_1_4.zip
You have chosen to open:
jmxdump_2015_1_4.zip
which is: WinRAR ZIP archive
from: http://localhost:8080
What should Firefox do with this file?
Open with
WinRAR archiver (default)
Save File
Do this automatically for files like this from now on.
OK
Cancel

Directories

Alfresco users and groups can be managed internally or we can integrate it with external directory servers such as LDAP, Active Directory, Kerberos, and so on. You can synchronize all the users and groups from this external directory in Alfresco. Note, no password information is stored in Alfresco if these external directories are used for authentication.

You can configure the chain of these external directories for authentication and synchronization. They would follow the same order as defined. This page allows you to configure and synchronize these external directories with Alfresco.

We would see more details about this configuration in *Chapter 6, Permissions and Security*.

Virtual filesystems

The content of Alfresco can be accessed as a virtual filesystem using CIFS/FTP. The Alfresco server can also be used as an IMAP server, you can just drag and drop e-mail content using this protocol. This page allows the administrator to configure and control these virtual filesystems.

All the configuration properties for CIFS, FTP, and IMAP, which we learned in *Chapter 3, Alfresco Configuration*, can have certain properties configured dynamically using this page. You can enable or disable the filesystems without a server restart.

Admin console in Alfresco Share

Share was designed as a collaboration platform in Alfresco. But since Alfresco version 5, on deprecation of Alfresco Explorer, Share is now the main interface for accessing the Alfresco repository. Some of the repository and Share administration operations are available using this admin console page.

To access the admin page in Share, follow these steps:

1. Log in to Alfresco Share `http://<IP>:<port>/share` using admin user credentials or via a user who is part of the `Alfresco_Administrator` group.
2. Click on **Admin Tools** in the right-most action in the top panel, as shown in the following screenshot. You will find various options to administer and control the Share GUI and repository.

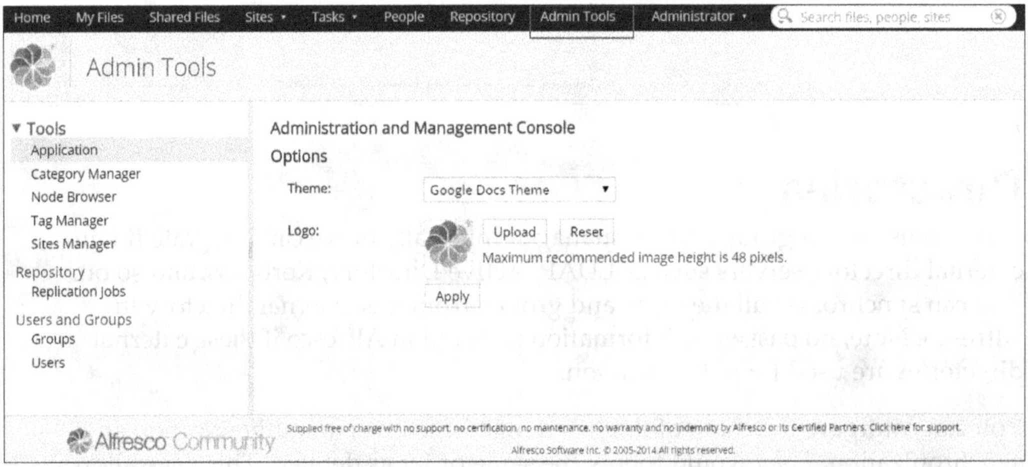

Home
My Files
Shared Files
Sites
Tasks
People
Repository
Admin Tools
Administrator
Search files, people, sites
Admin Tools
Tools
Application
Category Manager
Node Browser
Tag Manager
Sites Manager
Repository
Replication Jobs
Users and Groups
Groups
Users
Administration and Management Console
Options
Theme:
Google Docs Theme
Logo:
Upload
Reset
Maximum recommended image height is 48 pixels.
Apply
Alfresco Community
Supplied free of charge with no support, no certification, no maintenance, no warranty and no indemnity by Alfresco or its Certified Partners. Click here for support.
Alfresco Software Inc. © 2005-2014 All rights reserved.

> You can also directly access this admin page using this URL: `http://<IP>:<port>/share/page/console/admin-console/application`.

Let's see in detail each of the administrative operations available.

Application

This section provides control to modify the theme of the Share user interface. There are various default themes available in the drop-down menu, you can select any of them and apply. Also, the logo on the page can be changed.

Select the theme and upload a logo, as shown in the following screenshot, and hit **Apply**. Immediately the theme and logo will be changed.

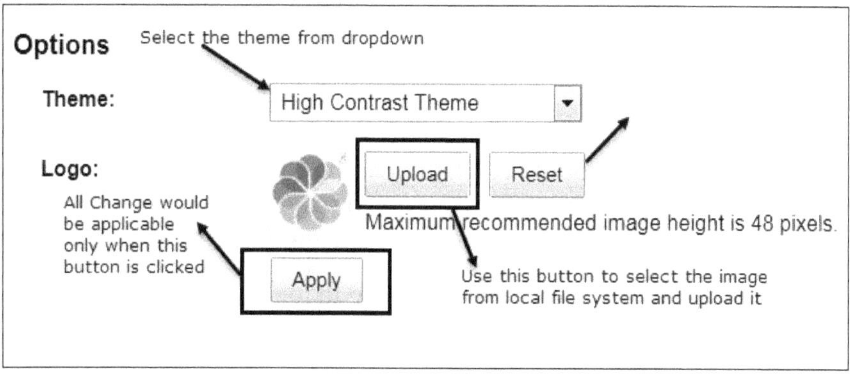
Options
Select the theme from dropdown
Theme:
High Contrast Theme
Logo:
Upload
Reset
All Change would be applicable only when this button is clicked
Maximum recommended image height is 48 pixels.
Apply
Use this button to select the image from local file system and upload it

Category Manager

Any content in Alfresco can be associated with a category. This page allows you to define new categories and manage existing ones. When you delete a category, it removes all the subcategories and also removes the link to any content that these categories were associated with.

Refer to the following screenshot, which shows details about how to manage these categories:

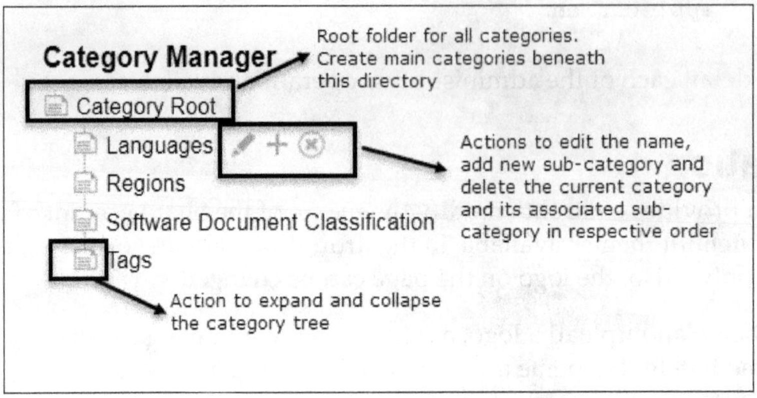
Category Manager
Root folder for all categories. Create main categories beneath this directory
Category Root
Languages
Regions
Software Document Classification
Tags
Actions to edit the name, add new sub-category and delete the current category and its associated sub-category in respective order
Action to expand and collapse the category tree

Node Browser

Node Browser is a very important tool for administrators for monitoring and troubleshooting purposes. This browser allows you to navigate through the complete repository and view details about every single individual node in the repository, either its folders, content, system folders, users, or groups. You can search content using Solr by using search queries. It also allows the interface to do a full text search.

For an administrator, this would be the first page to look for content if you want to troubleshoot a data issue in the repository.

Refer to the following screenshot for details about the Node Browser interface:

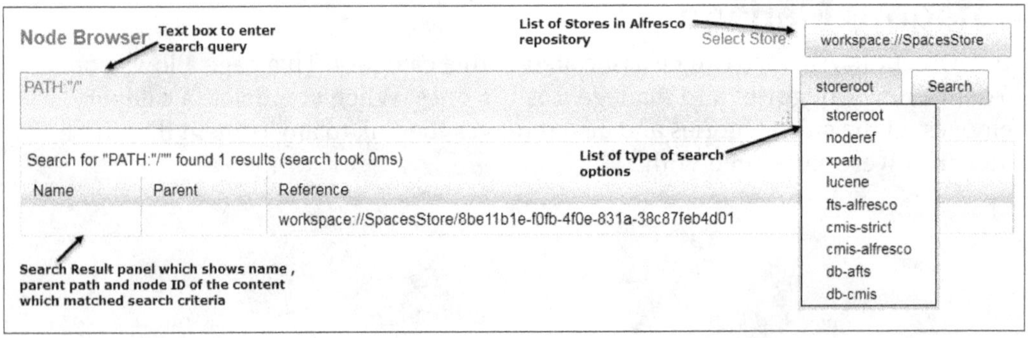
Node Browser
Text box to enter search query
List of Stores in Alfresco repository
Select Store:
workspace://SpacesStore
PATH:"/"
storeroot
Search
Search for "PATH:"/"" found 1 results (search took 0ms)
List of type of search options
Name
Parent
Reference
workspace://SpacesStore/8be11b1e-f0fb-4f0e-831a-38c87feb4d01
storeroot
noderef
xpath
lucene
fts-alfresco
cmis-strict
cmis-alfresco
db-afts
db-cmis
Search Result panel which shows name, parent path and node ID of the content which matched search criteria

Select Store drop-down list provides a list of stores available in Alfresco. In the Alfresco repository, the content is divided among different states based on type and state. Refer to the following screenshot for a full list of stores available.

Important ones are **workspace://SpacesStore**, as all the live content, folders, and system folders are under this store. All the archived content is under **archive:// SpacesStore**.

user://alfrescoUserStore as the name suggests contains details about the users in the repository.

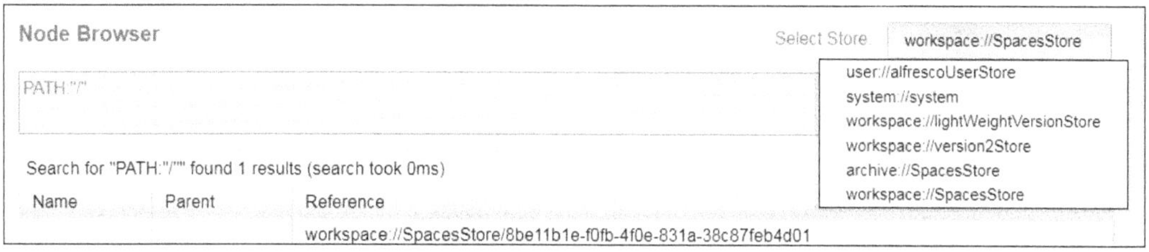
Node Browser
Select Store
workspace://SpacesStore
PATH:"/"
user://alfrescoUserStore
system://system
workspace://lightWeightVersionStore
workspace://version2Store
archive://SpacesStore
workspace://SpacesStore
Search for "PATH:"/"" found 1 results (search took 0ms)
Name
Parent
Reference
workspace://SpacesStore/8be11b1e-f0fb-4f0e-831a-38c87feb4d01

Let's see a different way to search content in Alfresco using this Node Browser:

- If you know the node ID and store information of any asset in Alfresco, you can easily find the node and its details using the **noderef** search option. Refer to the following screenshot:

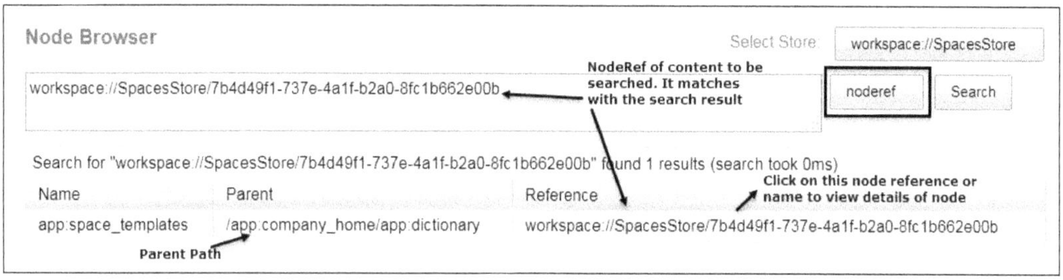
Node Browser
Select Store
workspace://SpacesStore
workspace://SpacesStore/7b4d49f1-737e-4a1f-b2a0-8fc1b662e00b
NodeRef of content to be searched. It matches with the search result
noderef
Search
Search for "workspace://SpacesStore/7b4d49f1-737e-4a1f-b2a0-8fc1b662e00b" found 1 results (search took 0ms)
Click on this node reference or name to view details of node
Name
Parent
Reference
app:space_templates
/app:company_home/app:dictionary
workspace://SpacesStore/7b4d49f1-737e-4a1f-b2a0-8fc1b662e00b
Parent Path

- Sometimes you don't know the node ID of the content and you want to navigate to the store, so you can use the **storeroot** option. This would give you the root node ID for the selected store and then you can navigate to that complete store. Refer to the following screenshot, which shows the root node ID for `workspace://SpacesStore`:

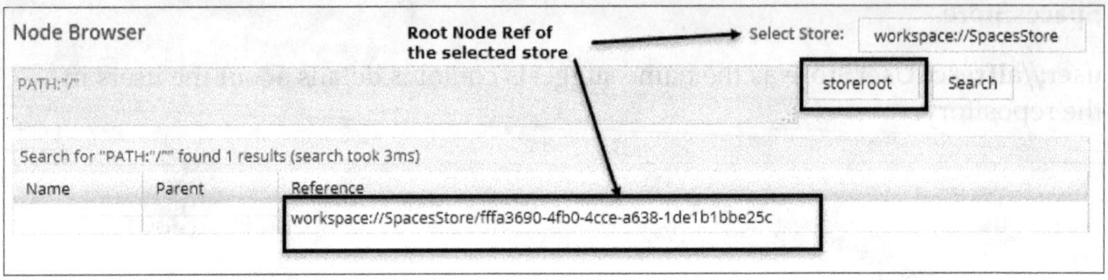
Node Browser
Root Node Ref of the selected store
Select Store:
workspace://SpacesStore
PATH:"/"
storeroot
Search
Search for "PATH:"/"" found 1 results (search took 3ms)
Name
Parent
Reference
workspace://SpacesStore/fffa3690-4fb0-4cce-a638-1de1b1bbe25c

- Alfresco also supports a full text search. Use the **fts-alfresco** option and provide the search text you are looking for. This would search for all the content in the selected store within the repository that contains the search term. Refer to the following screenshot:

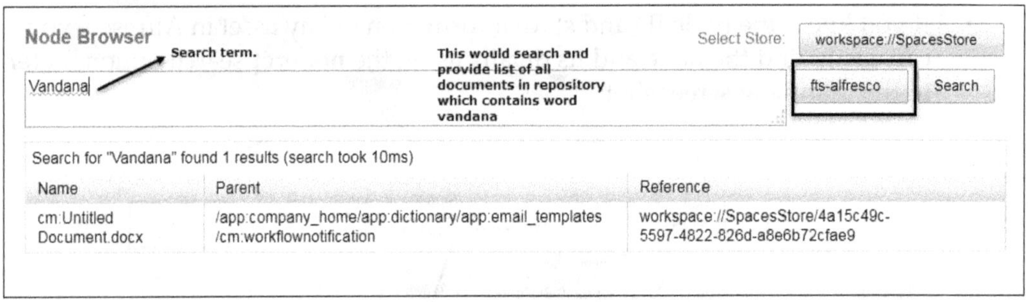
Node Browser
Search term.
This would search and provide list of all documents in repository which contains word vandana
Select Store:
workspace://SpacesStore
Vandana
fts-alfresco
Search
Search for "Vandana" found 1 results (search took 10ms)
Name
Parent
Reference
cm:Untitled Document.docx
/app:company_home/app:dictionary/app:email_templates /cm:workflownotification
workspace://SpacesStore/4a15c49c-5597-4822-826d-a8e6b72cfae9

- Using the **lucene** option you can search for content using the standard search queries. Alfresco provides some additional queries such as PATH and TYPE. Refer to the following screenshot to view details about the PATH query. Various search query details are covered in *Chapter 5, Search*.
- The following are some of the useful search queries that come in handy:
    - Search name of the content with a query such as, `@cm\:name:"Name of the content`.
    - Similarly you can search on any metadata of the content in the repository.
    - Search on type of content using a query such as, `TYPE:"cm:folder"`.

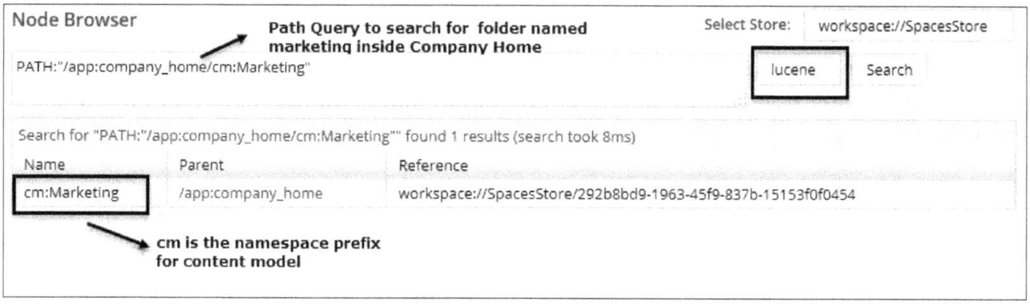
Node Browser
Path Query to search for folder named marketing inside Company Home
Select Store: workspace://SpacesStore
PATH:"/app:company_home/cm:Marketing"
lucene
Search
Search for "PATH:"/app:company_home/cm:Marketing"" found 1 results (search took 8ms)
Name
Parent
Reference
cm:Marketing
/app:company_home
workspace://SpacesStore/292b8bd9-1963-45f9-837b-15153f0f0454
cm is the namespace prefix for content model

- The CMIS query can also be executed in Node Browser to fetch the asset from the repository using the **cmis-alfresco** option.
- Once you get the search result, click on the node reference to view the details of the node. This page provides metadata, aspect, type details, children, permission, and a parent node reference. You can click on any children or parent node reference to navigate further. The following is a snapshot of the details page:

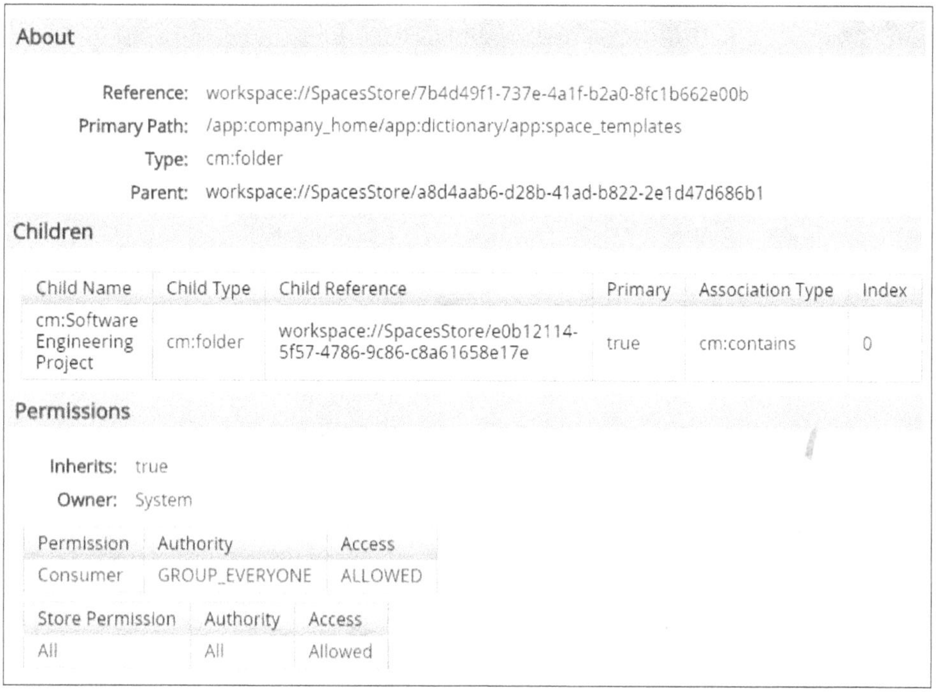
About
Reference: workspace://SpacesStore/7b4d49f1-737e-4a1f-b2a0-8fc1b662e00b
Primary Path: /app:company_home/app:dictionary/app:space_templates
Type: cm:folder
Parent: workspace://SpacesStore/a8d4aab6-d28b-41ad-b822-2e1d47d686b1
Children
Child Name
Child Type
Child Reference
Primary
Association Type
Index
cm:Software Engineering Project
cm:folder
workspace://SpacesStore/e0b12114-5f57-4786-9c86-c8a61658e17e
true
cm:contains
0
Permissions
Inherits: true
Owner: System
Permission
Authority
Access
Consumer
GROUP_EVERYONE
ALLOWED
Store Permission
Authority
Access
All
All
Allowed

Tag manager

Content in Alfresco can be tagged by the user. All the tags in the repository can be managed using this admin page. This tool also helps you to edit and delete the tag name.

For example, imagine a user created a tag named `marketing document` and associated it with thousands of documents. If later on we needed to update the tag to `marketing asset,` instead of updating thousands of documents, we just need to update the tag name using this page. All documents would have the updated tag.

The tag name in the search result has hyper links that would redirect to the document library and list all the documents that are tagged with the selected tag. So, if you find there is an unused tag, you can remove it from tag manager. This would help in maintaining a clean system.

Refer to the following screenshot, which shows details about tag manager:

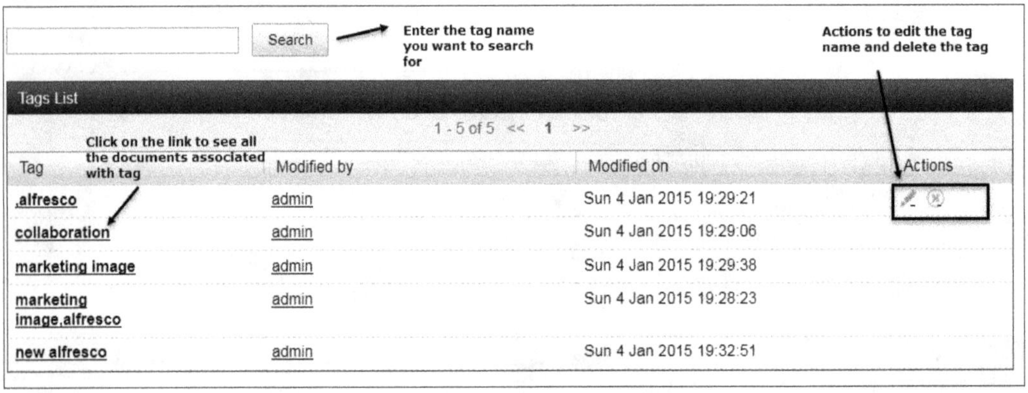
Search
Enter the tag name you want to search for
Actions to edit the tag name and delete the tag
Tags List
1 - 5 of 5 << 1 >>
Click on the link to see all the documents associated with tag
Tag
Modified by
Modified on
Actions
,alfresco
admin
Sun 4 Jan 2015 19:29:21
collaboration
admin
Sun 4 Jan 2015 19:29:06
marketing image
admin
Sun 4 Jan 2015 19:29:38
marketing image,alfresco
admin
Sun 4 Jan 2015 19:28:23
new alfresco
admin
Sun 4 Jan 2015 19:32:51

Site Manager

Users can create various public or private sites for collaboration. In earlier versions, there was no easy way to manage all these sites. Now, with the new version, the Site Manager tool helps administrators to keep full control and manage the sites effectively. The following screenshot show various types of sites, and the admin user is the Site Manager for all the sites:

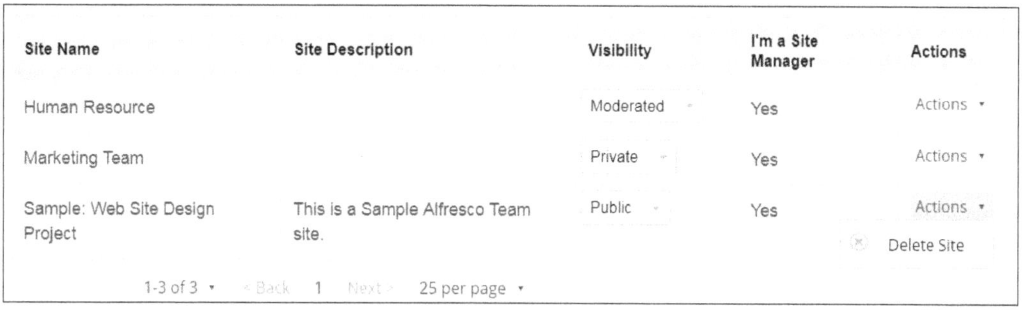
Site Name
Site Description
Visibility
I'm a Site Manager
Actions
Human Resource
Moderated
Yes
Actions
Marketing Team
Private
Yes
Actions
Sample: Web Site Design Project
This is a Sample Alfresco Team site.
Public
Yes
Actions
Delete Site
1-3 of 3
1
25 per page

Users

This page is the user administration of the repository. You can create, edit, or delete users from Alfresco. Alfresco also provides a feature to import a list of users using the `.csv` file.

Steps to create a new user in Alfresco

The following steps can be performed to create a new user in Alfresco:

1. Select **Users** in the admin tool in Share and click the **New User** button.
2. Fill in all the required details. You can also search for any group and add a user to any group at user creation time.

3. Click **Create User** or **Create and Create Another** (if you want to create more users). Refer to the following screenshot:

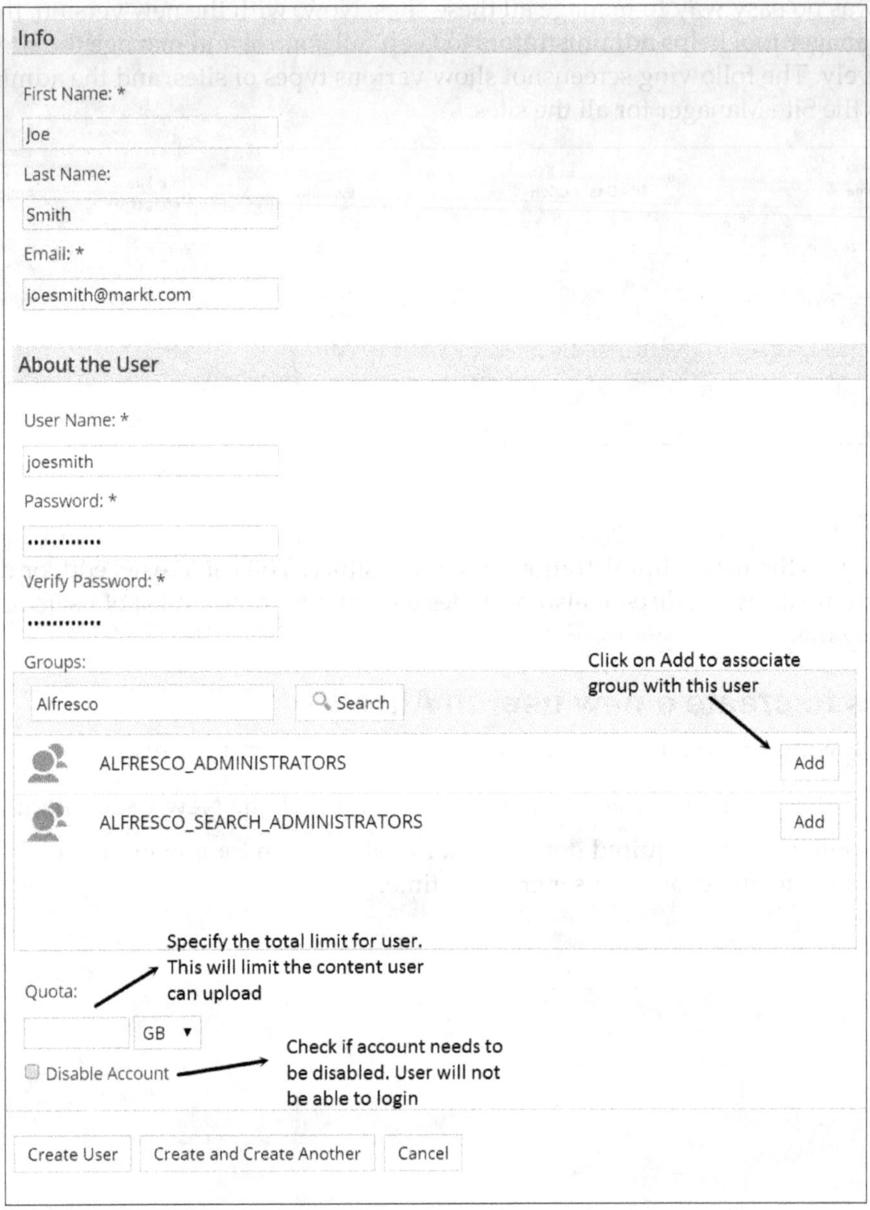
Info
First Name: *
Joe
Last Name:
Smith
Email: *
joesmith@markt.com
About the User
User Name: *
joesmith
Password: *
Verify Password: *
Groups:
Alfresco
Search
Click on Add to associate group with this user
ALFRESCO_ADMINISTRATORS
Add
ALFRESCO_SEARCH_ADMINISTRATORS
Add
Specify the total limit for user. This will limit the content user can upload
Quota:
GB
Disable Account
Check if account needs to be disabled. User will not be able to login
Create User
Create and Create Another
Cancel

Best practice would always be to bind the users to a group, if you know which group the user is going to be associated with.

Steps to edit and delete a user

The following steps can be performed to edit/delete a new user in Alfresco:

1. Select Users in the Share admin tool.
2. Search for the user you want to edit. For example, the Joe Smith user that we created lets us edit that user. The following screenshot shows details of the user search:

User Search
New User
Upload User CSV File
joe
Search
Search for "joe" found 1 results.
Name
User Name
Job Title
Email
Usage
Quota
Joe Smith
joesmith
joesmith@markt.com
0 bytes

3. Now click on user in the search result, this would redirect you to the details page of the user. Click on **Edit User** or **Delete User** based on the operation you want to perform.

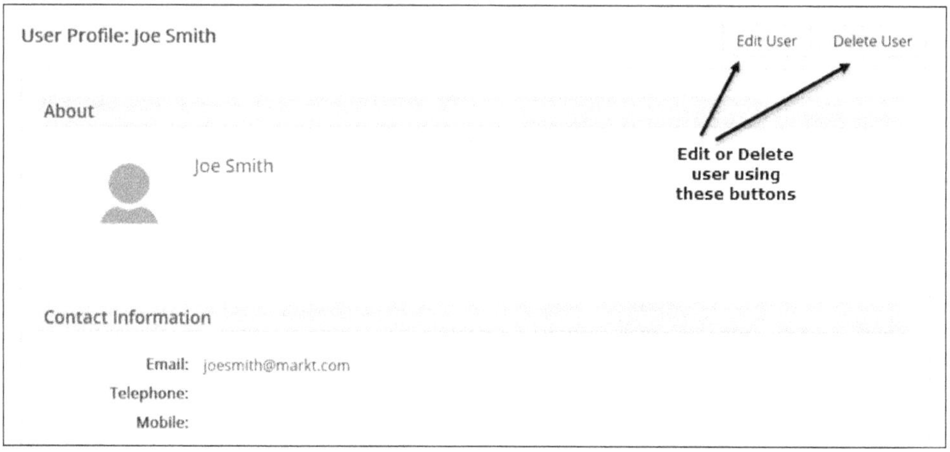
User Profile: Joe Smith
Edit User
Delete User
About
Joe Smith
Edit or Delete user using these buttons
Contact Information
Email: joesmith@markt.com
Telephone:
Mobile:

4. Be cautious when you do perform a delete operation on a user, since it cannot be restored. **Delete User** will remove the user from Alfresco completely. **Edit User** directs you to a details page where you can add or remove a user from a group, edit the password, and enable or disable the user account.

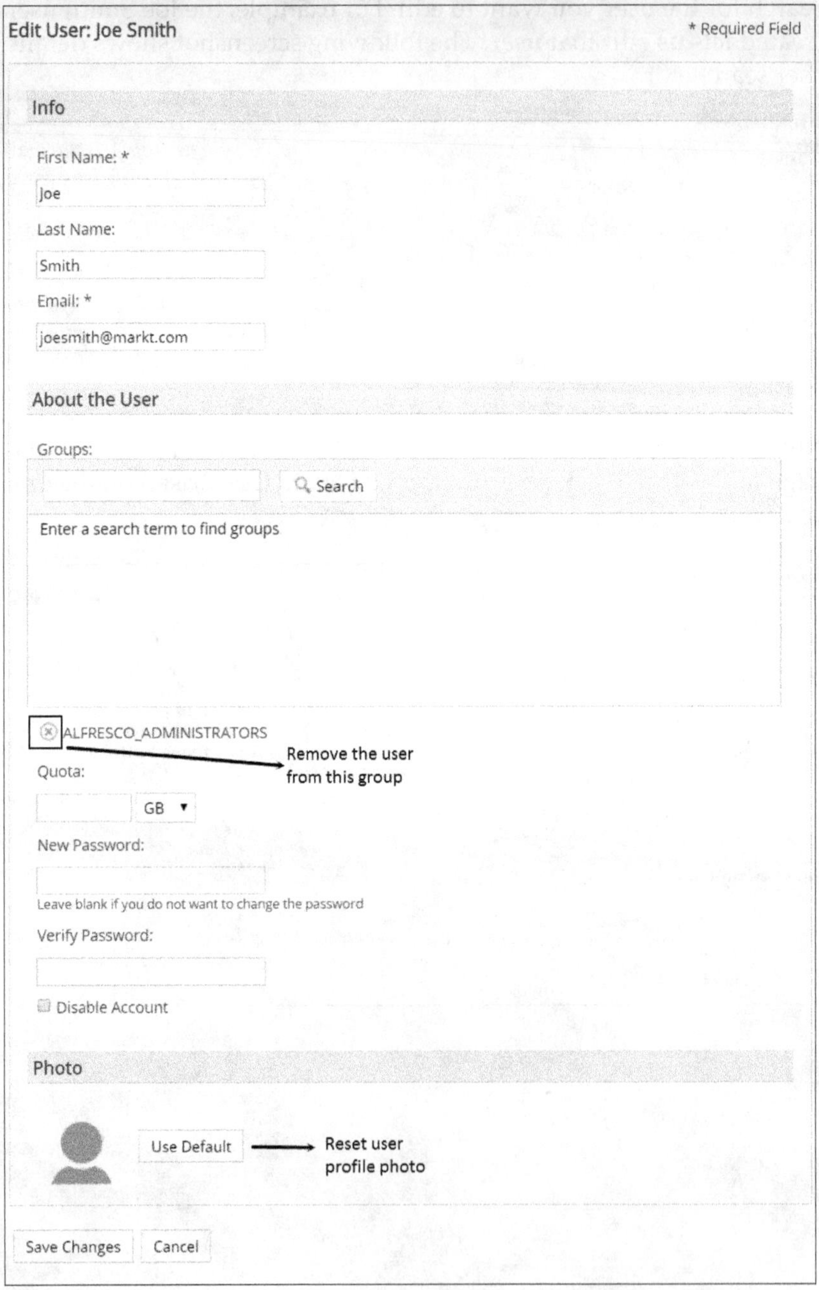
Edit User: Joe Smith
* Required Field
Info
First Name: *
Joe
Last Name:
Smith
Email: *
joesmith@markt.com
About the User
Groups:
Search
Enter a search term to find groups
ALFRESCO_ADMINISTRATORS
Remove the user from this group
Quota:
GB
New Password:
Leave blank if you do not want to change the password
Verify Password:
Disable Account
Photo
Use Default
Reset user profile photo
Save Changes
Cancel

Create multiple users using CSV File

The following steps can be performed to create multiple users in Alfresco:

1. Create a spreadsheet file with the `.csv` extension. Add a header as mentioned in the following and in the same order. Place the values for each of them. All fields are not mandatory:

   ```
   User Name,First Name,Last Name,E-mail
   Address,,Password,Company,Job Title,Location,Telephone,Mobile,Sky
   pe,IM,Google User Name,Address,Address Line 2,Address Line 3,Post
   Code,Telephone,Fax,Email
   ```

2. Open the **Users** page in **Admin Tools**.
3. Click on **Upload User CSV** file and browse for the `.csv` file created in step 1. Click **Upload File** to upload the `.csv` file. Once users are created you can see a list of users, and an e-mail will be sent to each individual user about their account details.

Group

Groups are a logical way to group a set of users. Specific permissions on folders or asset can be given to a group. So all the user members of that group will automatically inherit the same permission. This provides a better way to manage the security in the repository. If any user needs to be removed, just remove it from the group and all permissions would be revoked. No need to remove the user from tons of folders.

Always have a good naming convention for groups, so you can identify them easily. For example, if you want to group all HR people who have admin rights on a set of folders, name the group `HR_Admin`.

Once groups are created you cannot edit the name of the group. Only display names can be modified.

In Alfresco, you can also create sub-groups beneath root groups. Parent group permissions are automatically inherited by sub-groups. More details on permissions will be discussed in *Chapter 6, Permissions and Security*.

Group management is a very easy process. There is a simple user interface to perform this operation. Refer to the following screenshot for details:

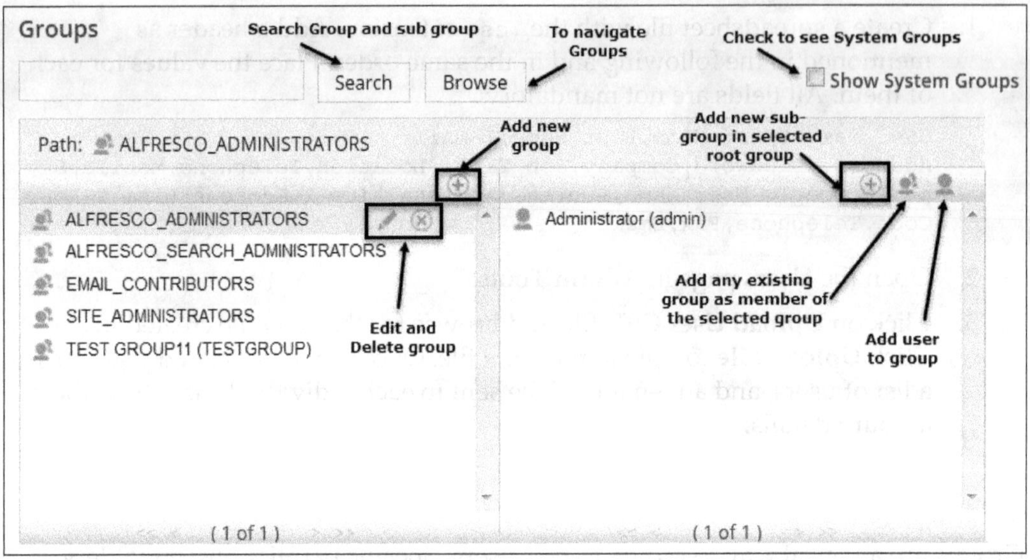
Groups
Search Group and sub group
To navigate Groups
Check to see System Groups
Search
Browse
Show System Groups
Path: ALFRESCO_ADMINISTRATORS
Add new group
Add new sub-group in selected root group
ALFRESCO_ADMINISTRATORS
ALFRESCO_SEARCH_ADMINISTRATORS
EMAIL_CONTRIBUTORS
SITE_ADMINISTRATORS
TEST GROUP11 (TESTGROUP)
Edit and Delete group
Administrator (admin)
Add any existing group as member of the selected group
Add user to group
(1 of 1)
(1 of 1)

Admin console in Alfresco Explorer

Alfresco Explorer is one of the web-client interfaces that provides document management and administration capabilities. It is being deprecated from Alfresco version 5.0.

Follow these steps to access the administrator console of Alfresco Explorer:

1. Log in to Alfresco Explorer (`http://<ip>:<port>/alfresco`) using your admin credentials. You need to log in with an administrator username. The default administrator username is `admin`. Any user that is part of the `Alfresco_Administrator` group, will also have the same admin rights. We will see in a later section of this chapter how to add users to groups.

2. Click on the **Administration Console** icon in the upper-right corner of the **My Dashboard** page. It opens the admin console options as shown in the following screenshot:

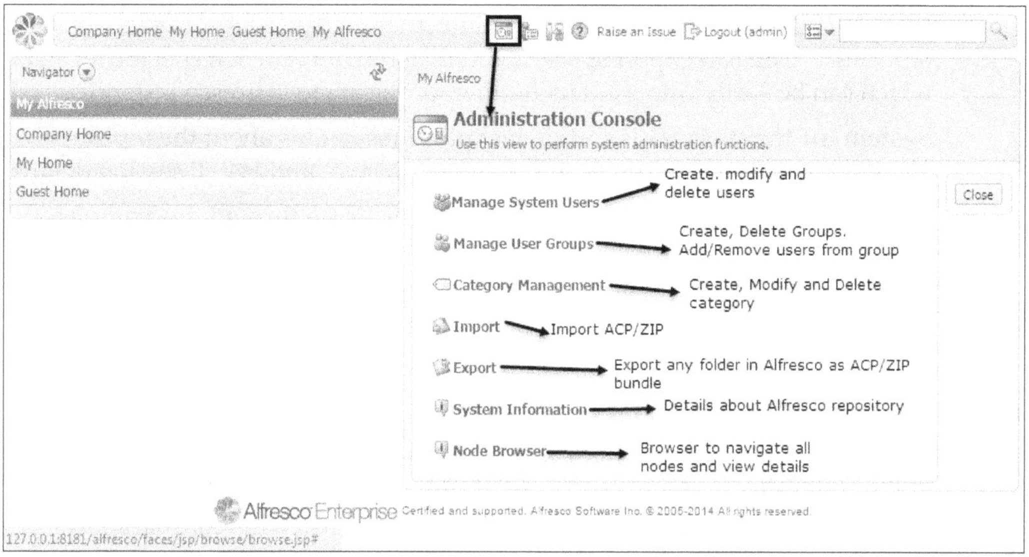
Company Home My Home Guest Home My Alfresco
Raise an Issue
Logout (admin)
Navigator
My Alfresco
Company Home
My Home
Guest Home
My Alfresco
Administration Console
Use this view to perform system administration functions.
Close
Manage System Users
Create, modify and delete users
Manage User Groups
Create, Delete Groups. Add/Remove users from group
Category Management
Create, Modify and Delete category
Import
Import ACP/ZIP
Export
Export any folder in Alfresco as ACP/ZIP bundle
System Information
Details about Alfresco repository
Node Browser
Browser to navigate all nodes and view details
Alfresco Enterprise
127.0.0.1:8181/alfresco/faces/jsp/browse/browse.jsp#

Alfresco Explorer provides the following options of administration:

- **Manage System Users**: As the name suggests, this option allows you to manage users of the repository. It allows you to create, modify, and delete users. It also allows you to change a password for any user in the repository. It is the same as what we covered in the Share user admin console. The only difference here is you cannot add a user to a group while creating or editing user information.
- **Manage User Groups**: As the name suggests, this is to manage groups in Alfresco. Groups are a logical grouping of users and sub-groups. You can create/delete groups, and add/remove users from groups.
- **Category Management**: In Alfresco you can categorize the content/folder by associating them with any category. This section allows you to create/delete different categories that can be associated with any space or content in Alfresco.

- **Import**: This administrative action allows you to import information from one repository to the same or another Alfresco repository. You can import space, content, and its associated metadata in the same format from another Alfresco instance.
- **Export**: This allows you to export the information from the Alfresco repository. You can export space, content, and metadata in a specific format, which can be easily imported in another, or the same, Alfresco instance.
- **System Information**: This section just provides details about the repository and system information such as Tomcat path, Java, and HTTP session details.
- **Node Browser**: This browser allows you to navigate through the complete repository. It also allows you to search any node based on the *Node-ref* or search query. It is the same as what we saw in an earlier part of this book in Share admin tools.

Activiti workflow console

Workflows in Alfresco use the Activiti engine. Activiti workflow also provides its own workflow console to monitor and manage the workflows in Alfresco. This is a very user-friendly interface to show details about workflows. This console shows the list of workflows deployed and running process instance. It also shows all the database tables used by Activiti.

Log in with Alfresco admin credentials using the URL; `http://<IP>:<port>/alfresco/activiti-admin` to access the workflow console.

There are various pages to this workflow console. Let's go through each of them in detail:

- **Deployments**: This section shows the list of deployed workflows. It shows details of when the last deployment was done for each of the workflows. The link is provided to access the process definition XML and diagram. It also provides an option to upload a new process definition as a `.zip` or `bpmn20.xml` file.

- **Deployed process definitions**: This section shows details about the process definitions in the repository. Process definitions, as the name suggests, define the complete flow from start to end. Let's say for a simple Approve Reject workflow, this process definition will define the start point, how many steps are required in the process, and what the percentage of approval or rejection before marking a final status of completion of the workflow should be. Process instance is a running instance of process definitions. In simple terms, like having a Java class and different objects of the same class. There can be multiple process instances for the same definitions. The process instance will be in a state at any point of time. You can see a complete process diagram for each of the deployed process definitions in Alfresco, and if there are any active process instances for that workflow, you will see the list of IDs. As shown in the following diagram, there is a simple parallel review and approve process diagram. There is one active workflow, which you can see in the process instance section. Click on **view** to see the process instance details.

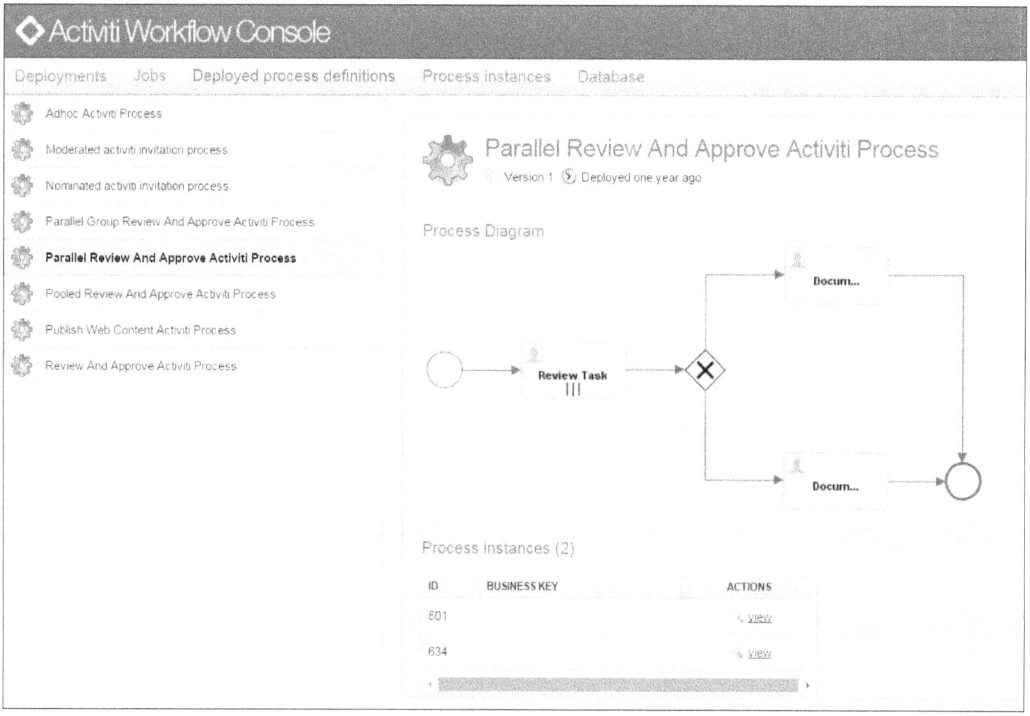
Activiti Workflow Console
Deployments
Jobs
Deployed process definitions
Process instances
Database
Adhoc Activiti Process
Moderated activiti invitation process
Nominated activiti invitation process
Parallel Group Review And Approve Activiti Process
Parallel Review And Approve Activiti Process
Pooled Review And Approve Activiti Process
Publish Web Content Activiti Process
Review And Approve Activiti Process
Parallel Review And Approve Activiti Process
Version 1
Deployed one year ago
Process Diagram
Review Task
Docum...
Docum...
Process instances (2)
ID
BUSINESS KEY
ACTIONS
501
view
634
view

- **Process instances**: This page shows details about the active processes. You can see there was an active workflow instance in the preceding diagram for parallel review and process. When you click on **view** it takes you to the process instance page with more details about the workflow. It shows the current state in the process diagram. You can also delete the active process instance using the delete action provided in the upper-right corner of the page.

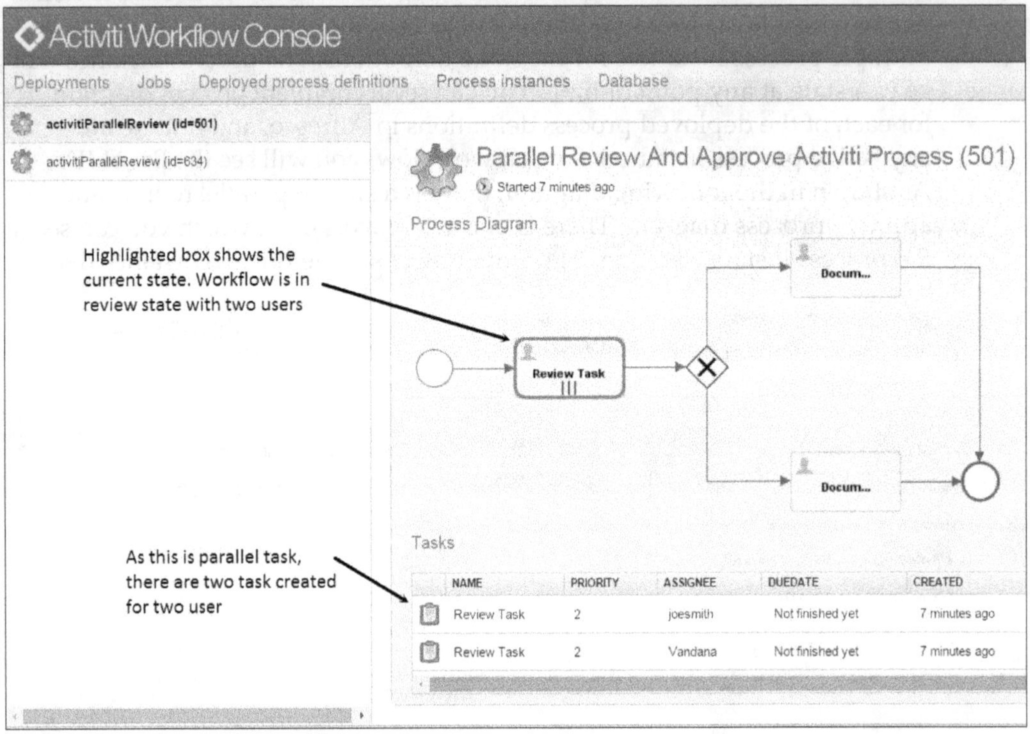
Activiti Workflow Console
Deployments
Jobs
Deployed process definitions
Process instances
Database
activitiParallelReview (id=501)
activitiParallelReview (id=634)
Parallel Review And Approve Activiti Process (501)
Started 7 minutes ago
Process Diagram
Highlighted box shows the current state. Workflow is in review state with two users
Review Task
Docum...
Docum...
Tasks
As this is parallel task, there are two task created for two user
NAME
PRIORITY
ASSIGNEE
DUEDATE
CREATED
Review Task
2
joesmith
Not finished yet
7 minutes ago
Review Task
2
Vandana
Not finished yet
7 minutes ago

- **Database**: This section shows all the database tables of Alfresco, which are specifically for the Activiti workflow. It also shows the count and all the rows of the data. This count will be useful to get the workflow statistic in Alfresco during the upgrade process.

> For more details about business processes you can refer to `https://en.wikipedia.org/wiki/Business_Process_Model_and_Notation`.

Summary

Alfresco provides a very easy user interface to administrate and monitor the repository. This chapter helped you to understand about the various admin consoles available, specific to the system. Standalone admin consoles are for configuring the Alfresco system.

The Share admin console is used to manage users, groups, tags, categories, and sites. It also allows you to change the look and feel of the Share interface.

Node Browser is one of the very important tools for admin and developers, which allows users to look up any node and its details in the repository. Node Browser is a really handy tool while troubleshooting Alfresco. Also a note here, there are certain admin console changes in Alfresco v 5.1.

In the next chapter we will talk in detail about search engines in Alfresco. Details such as how to manage them, configure them, and tune them will be discussed.

5
Search

The function of a search in any ECM system is to allow the user to search all content in the repository which users have access to. Here, in Alfresco, search is a combination of searching content along with permission control. In most ECM systems, search is supported via a search engine. The responsibility of a search engine is to index the content in the repository and provide the user with search query capability to search content. Certain search engines work in a synchronized way: content is indexed immediately as it enters the repository. In some search engines, content is indexed in an asynchronized way.

One of the biggest features of Alfresco 5.x is search. The new Solr4 search engine was introduced in the latest version of Alfresco. In the old version of Alfresco, it used to have old versions of Solr and Lucene as its search engines. Alfresco allows users to search any content they have access to in the repository. Alfresco supports both full text and metadata searches.

We will cover the following topics in this chapter:

- Understanding Solr and Alfresco integration
- Configuring and managing Solr
- Troubleshooting Solr

Understanding Solr and Alfresco integration

Searching in Alfresco is supported via the Solr4 search engine. Solr4 works as a standalone enterprise application. It is built in Java and uses `lucene` internally for indexing. Solr extends the `lucene` library to add new features around it and make it a standalone application. It exposes the REST API for searching and submitting content for indexing. It supports the indexing of any data via JSON/XML/CSV or binary. The search request is also supported by a HTTP Get request. Using HTTP, GET data can be searched using Solr.

Solr4 can be installed as an integral application with Alfresco on the same application server or it can be installed completely on a separate machine. The latest version of Solr4 also supports the clustering and sharding of indexing.

There are various advantages of Solr:

- Scalable
- Better performance
- Allows Facet search and more accurate results
- Easy monitoring and administration
- Asynchronous indexing near to real time
- Compact disk formats
- Alfresco and Solr communicate with each other via HTTP asynchronously.

Solr polls Alfresco at certain intervals to fetch all transactional information for indexing. This transactional data includes node information and permission information. Solr also polls the data model from Alfresco to define the schema for indexing. As you know, in Alfresco there are two stores: `workspaceStore` (live content) and `archiveStore` (archived content). Solr creates different sets of indexes for both stores and has different configurations for each of them.

Installing Solr

Solr can be installed via the Alfresco installation wizard within Alfresco. In this case, both Alfresco and Solr will be in the same application server. By default, Solr4 will be enabled. But if you are installing Alfresco in an application server other than Tomcat, you have to install Solr4 separately on Tomcat. Also, as the indexing process is memory- and CPU-intensive, it is always recommended to install Solr on a different machine to Alfresco.

Let's go through the steps to install Solr as an independent application on a Tomcat server.

Before we dive into the detail, let's consider that `ALFRESCO_HOME` and `SOLR_HOME` are two directories where Alfresco and Solr are installed. Both are installed in separate Tomcat servers.

For example:

- `ALFRESCO_HOME = /opt/alfresco`
- `SOLR_HOME = /opt/solr`

The installation steps are as follows:

1. Install the Tomcat application based on the Alfresco supported platform. Download the Tomcat core binary distribution from `http://tomcat.apache.org`. Unpack the binary distribution so that it resides in the directory `<SOLR_HOME>/tomcat`. Always go through the Alfresco-supported stack list before deciding on the platform.
2. Download the Alfresco enterprise download ZIP bundle from the Alfresco-supported stack and extract the bundle. Only valid Alfresco subscription users can download the resources of the enterprise edition from the Alfresco Customer Support portal. Another option is a 30 day trial version which can be downloaded by submitting the online form.
3. Assuming Alfresco is already installed without Solr4, now copy the `Solr4` directory from the extracted bundle under `<SOLR_HOME>`.
4. Copy the `solr4.war` file from `<Extracted_Directory>/web-server/webapps` under `<SOLR_HOME>/tomcat/webapps`.
5. Copy the `context.xml` file from `<SOLR_HOME>/solr4` to `<SOLR_HOME>/tomcat/conf/Catalina/localhost/solr4.xml`.
6. Edit `solrcore.properties` in `<SOLR_HOME>/solr4/workspace-SpacesStore/conf/` and `<SOLR_HOME>/solr4/archive-SpacesStore/conf/` to point to the proper Alfresco server and index location. Modify the following listed properties:
    - `data.dir.root=@@ALFRESCO_SOLR4_DATA_DIR@@`< Make sure this points to the directory where the index will be created. For example, `<SOLR_HOME>/alf_data/solr4/index`>
    - `alfresco.host=localhost`< Provide the host address of the Alfresco server>
    - `alfresco.port=8080`< Port on which Alfresco is running>

 - alfresco.port.ssl=8443
 - alfresco.baseUrl=/alfresco
 - alfresco.cron=0/15 * * * * ? *

7. Edit the `solr4.xml` file to make sure the environment variables are pointing to the correct location. Sample entries are shown in the code snippet below. You have to make sure this directory exists and the user starting the Solr application has access to read and write to this directory:

```
<Environment name="solr/home" type="java.lang.String" value="/opt/
solr4" override="true"/>
<Environment name="solr/model/dir" type="java.lang.String"
value="/opt/solr4/alf_data/model" override="true"/>
<Environment name="solr/content/dir" type="java.lang.String"
value="/opt/solr4/alf_data/content" override="true"/>
```

8. As both Alfresco and Solr communicates via HTTPS trusted certificates, they need to be installed on both servers for handshaking.
9. Copy the `keystore` directory from <Extracted_Directory>/alf_data on both the Alfresco and Solr servers in the `alf_data` directory. Your folder structure will look something like this <ALFRESCO_HOME>/alf_data/keystore and <SOLR_HOME>/alf_data/keystore.
10. From a security standpoint, it is important to generate your own keys for secure communication between Alfresco and Solr. There is already a script provided: "`generate_keystores.sh`" file under the <ALFRESCO_HOME>/alf_data/keystore directory.
11. Edit the `generate_keystores.sh` file and make sure the properties listed below are set properly:

```
ALFRESCO_HOME - Home Directory of Alfresco. For example "/opt/
alfresco"

ALFRESCO_KEYSTORE_HOME - Keystore path in Alfresco , for example
"/opt/alfresco/alf_data/keystore"
SOLR_HOME - Directory path where solr is installed, for example "/
opt/solr/solr4"
JAVA_HOME - Java home location
REPO_CERT_DNAME - Provide proper repository certificate domain
name
SOLR_CLIENT_CERT_DNAME - Provide proper solr client certificate
domain name
```

12. Execute the script on the Alfresco server and copy the same cert on the Solr server under <SOLR_HOME>/alf_data/keystore. Also copy the Solr related certificate under <SOLR_HOME>/solr4/workspace-SpacesStore/conf and <SOLR_HOME>/solr4/archive-SpacesStore/conf.
13. Configure tomcat/conf/server.xml in both <ALFRESCO_HOME> and <SOLR_HOME> for HTTPS connector port 8443, as shown in the following code snippet. Make sure the keystorepass and truststorepass are set to the password used during the keystore generation process:

```
<Connector port="8443" URIEncoding="UTF-8" protocol="org.apache.
coyote.http11.Http11Protocol" SSLEnabled="true" maxThreads="150"
scheme="https" keystoreFile="<ALFRESCO_HOME/SOLR_HOME> /
alf_data/keystore/ssl.keystore" keystorePass="kT9X6oe68t"
keystoreType="JCEKS" secure="true" connectionTimeout="240000"
truststoreFile="<ALFRESCO_HOME/SOLR_HOME>/alf_data/keystore/ssl.
truststore" truststorePass="kT9X6oe68t" truststoreType="JCEKS"
clientAuth="want" sslProtocol="TLS" allowUnsafeLegacyRenegotiation
="true" maxHttpHeaderSize="32768" />
```

14. Configure the Alfresco server identity in the Solr server by adding the line below in the <SOLR_HOME>/tomcat/conf/tomcat-users.xml file. If you have created a custom domain during the certificate generation process, make sure this entry matches with REPO_CERT_DNAME:

```
<user username="CN=Alfresco Repository, OU=Unknown, O=Alfresco
Software Ltd., L=Maidenhead, ST=UK, C=GB" roles="repository"
password="null"/>
```

15. In a similar way, configure the Solr server identity in the Alfresco server by adding the line below in the <ALFRESCO_HOME>/tomcat/conf/tomcat-users.xml file. If you have created a custom domain during the certificate generation process, make sure this entry matches with SOLR_CLIENT_CERT_DNAME:

```
<user username="CN=Alfresco Repository Client, OU=Unknown,
O=Alfresco Software Ltd., L=Maidenhead, ST=UK, C=GB"
roles="repoclient" password="null"/>
```

16. Configure the alfresco-global.properties file in <ALFRESCO_HOME>/tomcat/shared/classes to point to the correct Solr server and keystore directory. Add or edit the following set of properties:
    - index.subsystem.name=solr4<Search Subsystem name. This will remain as solr4>
    - solr.host=localhost<Specify Solr host address>
    - solr.port=8080<Solr Non SSL port>
    - solr.port.ssl=8443<Solr SSL port>
    - dir.keystore=${dir.root}/keystore<Alfresco keystore path used for https communication with Solr>

17. You can enable Solr in Alfresco via the admin console, as shown in the following screenshot, or by using JMX:

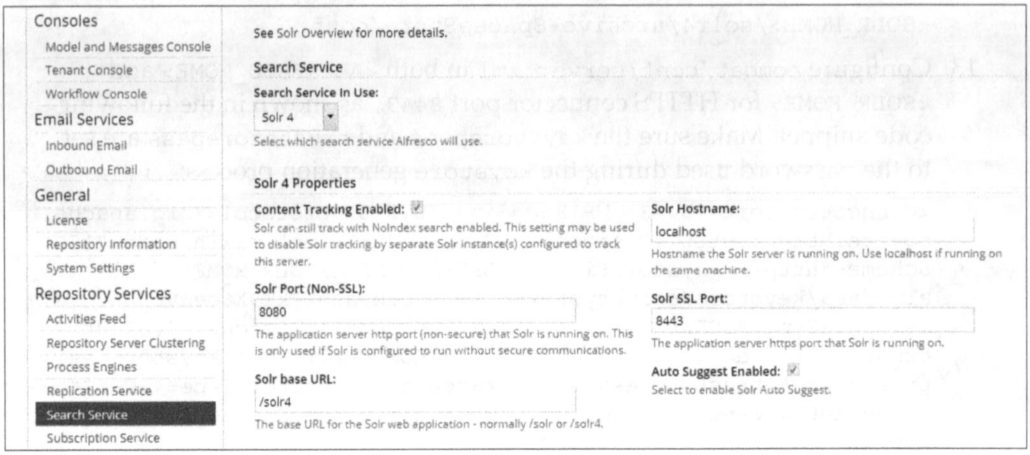
Consoles
Model and Messages Console
Tenant Console
Workflow Console
Email Services
Inbound Email
Outbound Email
General
License
Repository Information
System Settings
Repository Services
Activities Feed
Repository Server Clustering
Process Engines
Replication Service
Search Service
Subscription Service
See Solr Overview for more details.
Search Service
Search Service In Use:
Solr 4
Select which search service Alfresco will use.
Solr 4 Properties
Content Tracking Enabled:
Solr can still track with NoIndex search enabled. This setting may be used to disable Solr tracking by separate Solr instance(s) configured to track this server.
Solr Hostname:
localhost
Hostname the Solr server is running on. Use localhost if running on the same machine.
Solr Port (Non-SSL):
8080
The application server http port (non-secure) that Solr is running on. This is only used if Solr is configured to run without secure communications.
Solr SSL Port:
8443
The application server https port that Solr is running on.
Auto Suggest Enabled:
Select to enable Solr Auto Suggest.
Solr base URL:
/solr4
The base URL for the Solr web application - normally /solr or /solr4.

18. Start the Alfresco and Solr server.

Understanding the Solr directory structure

Once the Solr server is installed properly, there are various directories and files which are important for an admin to understand from a proper maintenance and configuration standpoint. There are two main directories under `<SOLR_HOME>`, one is Solr4 which contains all the configuration for Solr, and another is `alf_data/solr4`, which actually stores the indexes, models, and content fetched from Alfresco.

Let's go through the important files in detail. Considering everything under `<SOLR_HOME>`:

- `alf_data/solr4/model`: This directory contains all the data models of Alfresco. Solr pulls this information from the Alfresco server in certain intervals for indexing purposes.
- `alf_data/solr4/index`: This directory has two sub-folders: `workspace` and `archive`. Each folder stores indexes respective to each store.
- `solr4`: This directory contains the configuration related to indexing and Alfresco communication. It contains two sub-directories for each store. All configuration files are present for each store.

- `solr4/<store>/core.properties`: This property defines the name of the core.
- `solr4<store>/conf/solrconfig.xml`: This is the main Solr configuration `.xml` file. All index, search, and facet related configuration is present in this file. Edit this file only if you have a proper understanding of the impact of the changes.
- `solr4/<store>/conf/schema.xml`: As the name suggests, this file contains the schema of the fields defined for Alfresco.
- `solr4/<store>/conf/solrcore.properties`: This file contains important configuration related to index location, Alfresco connection details, and SSL certificate information.

Administration and monitoring of Solr

There are various methods to administrate and monitor the Solr server. You can use either the Alfresco admin console to track the indexing status or the enable/disable search service. Solr also has its own built-in admin page. The Solr admin page provides full health indexes. Let's go through each of the different sections.

Understanding the Alfresco search admin console

As covered in Chapter 4, *Administration of Alfresco*, Alfresco has its own admin console. Within this admin console, there is a section named **Search Service**. It is again divided into different sections in order to configure and monitor Solr. The admin console can be accessed via `http://<alfresco ip address>:<port>/alfresco/s/enterprise/admin`:

- **Search Service**: As shown in the following screenshot, it has a dropdown with three values: **Solr**, **Solr4**, and **No Index**. **Solr** is the old Solr subsystem and this should be enabled only during the upgrade process from older versions of Alfresco. The **Solr4** subsystem is the one, which should be enabled by default. **No Index** turns off the search engine and all requests for search is passed to the database:

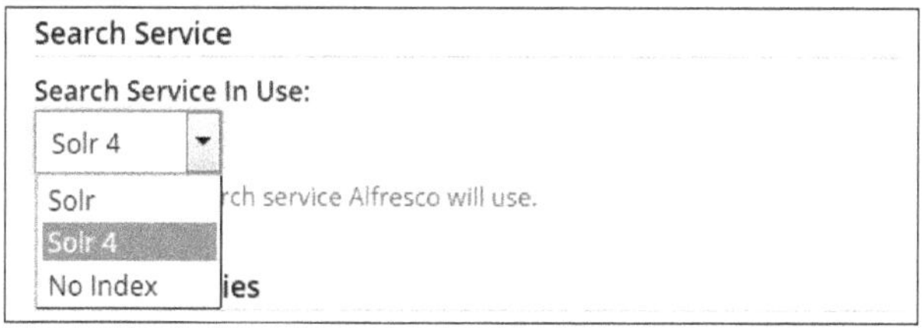
Search Service
Search Service In Use:
Solr 4
Solr
Solr 4
No Index

- **Store Tracking Status**: This section shows the Solr indexing tracking status for both stores. It provides information about the last transaction indexed. In Alfresco, all indexing is tracked via transaction. Each transaction refers to a set of nodes in the repository updated during that transaction. As shown in the following screenshot, it also shows the memory usage and disk usage by Solr.

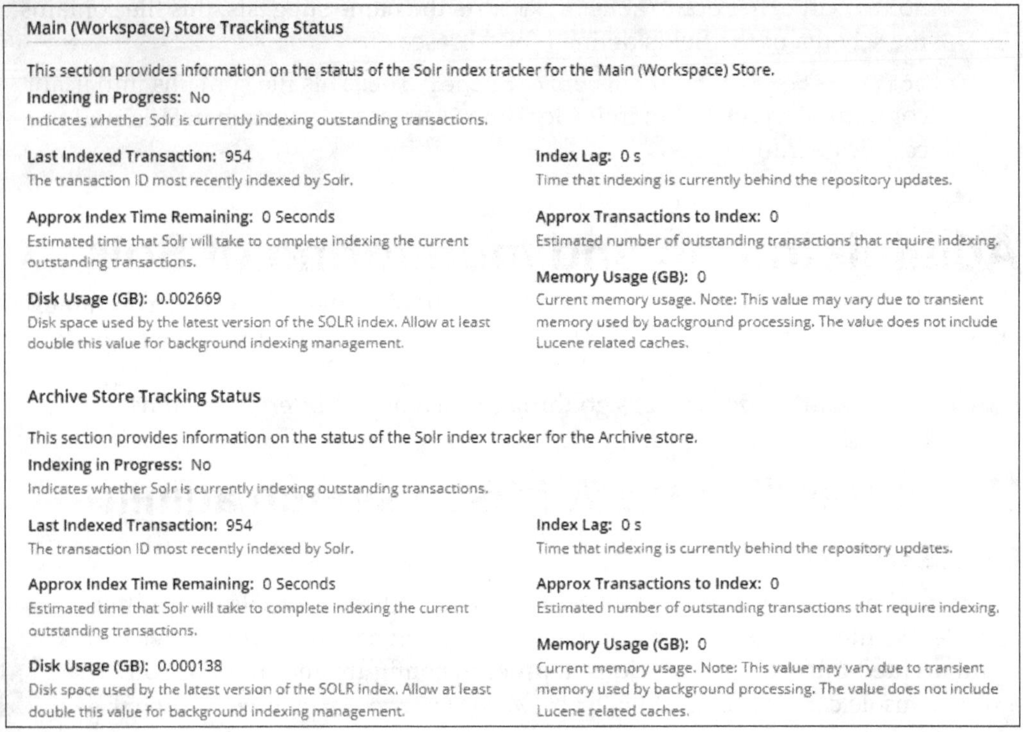
Main (Workspace) Store Tracking Status
This section provides information on the status of the Solr index tracker for the Main (Workspace) Store.
Indexing in Progress: No
Indicates whether Solr is currently indexing outstanding transactions.
Last Indexed Transaction: 954
The transaction ID most recently indexed by Solr.
Index Lag: 0 s
Time that indexing is currently behind the repository updates.
Approx Index Time Remaining: 0 Seconds
Estimated time that Solr will take to complete indexing the current outstanding transactions.
Approx Transactions to Index: 0
Estimated number of outstanding transactions that require indexing.
Memory Usage (GB): 0
Current memory usage. Note: This value may vary due to transient memory used by background processing. The value does not include Lucene related caches.
Disk Usage (GB): 0.002669
Disk space used by the latest version of the SOLR index. Allow at least double this value for background indexing management.
Archive Store Tracking Status
This section provides information on the status of the Solr index tracker for the Archive store.
Indexing in Progress: No
Indicates whether Solr is currently indexing outstanding transactions.
Last Indexed Transaction: 954
The transaction ID most recently indexed by Solr.
Index Lag: 0 s
Time that indexing is currently behind the repository updates.
Approx Index Time Remaining: 0 Seconds
Estimated time that Solr will take to complete indexing the current outstanding transactions.
Approx Transactions to Index: 0
Estimated number of outstanding transactions that require indexing.
Memory Usage (GB): 0
Current memory usage. Note: This value may vary due to transient memory used by background processing. The value does not include Lucene related caches.
Disk Usage (GB): 0.000138
Disk space used by the latest version of the SOLR index. Allow at least double this value for background indexing management.

- **Backup Settings**: This section allows the administrator to configure the backup of Solr indexes for both stores. The administrator can provide the backup location, scheduled backup time, and the number of backups to be kept. This backup process will only be applicable if your Solr server is installed within the Alfresco server.

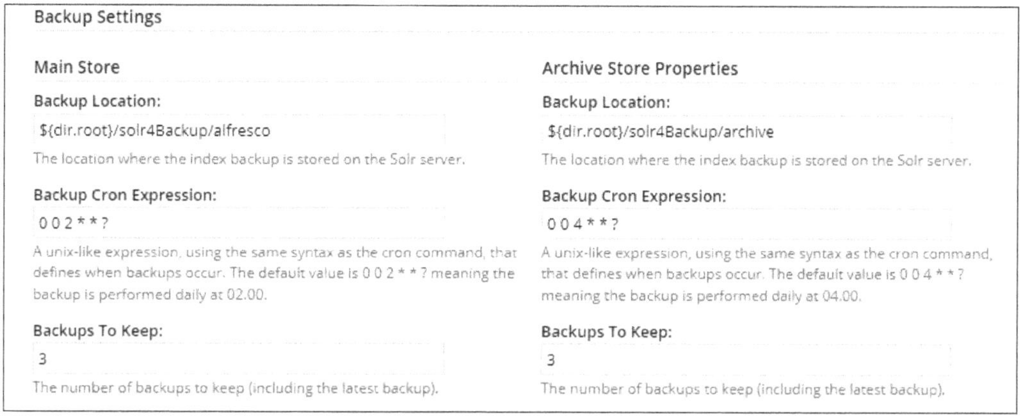
Backup Settings
Main Store
Backup Location:
${dir.root}/solr4Backup/alfresco
The location where the index backup is stored on the Solr server.
Backup Cron Expression:
0 0 2 * * ?
A unix-like expression, using the same syntax as the cron command, that defines when backups occur. The default value is 0 0 2 * * ? meaning the backup is performed daily at 02.00.
Backups To Keep:
3
The number of backups to keep (including the latest backup).
Archive Store Properties
Backup Location:
${dir.root}/solr4Backup/archive
The location where the index backup is stored on the Solr server.
Backup Cron Expression:
0 0 4 * * ?
A unix-like expression, using the same syntax as the cron command, that defines when backups occur. The default value is 0 0 4 * * ? meaning the backup is performed daily at 04.00.
Backups To Keep:
3
The number of backups to keep (including the latest backup).

Understanding the Solr admin console

Solr as a standalone application provides its own admin console. This admin console has all the details related to Solr server and indexes. It shows you the full health of the indexes. If Solr instances are clustered, this single browser-based admin page will be helpful when tracking each of the nodes.

As the Solr server can only be accessed via HTTPS, you have to import the client certificate in your browser before accessing the Solr admin page. In Firefox, navigate to **Options** | **Advanced** | **View Certificates**. Click on **Import** under the **Your Certificate** tab. Browse to the `browser.p12` certificate located in `<ALFRESCO_HOME>/alf_data/keystore`. Set the password as `alfresco` and save this certificate.

Access the URL below from your browser, a prompt will appear regarding an unsecured certificate, click on **Add Exception** and proceed. This will take you to the main dashboard page, as shown in the following screenshot. Navigate to `http://<solr server ip address>:8443/solr4`:

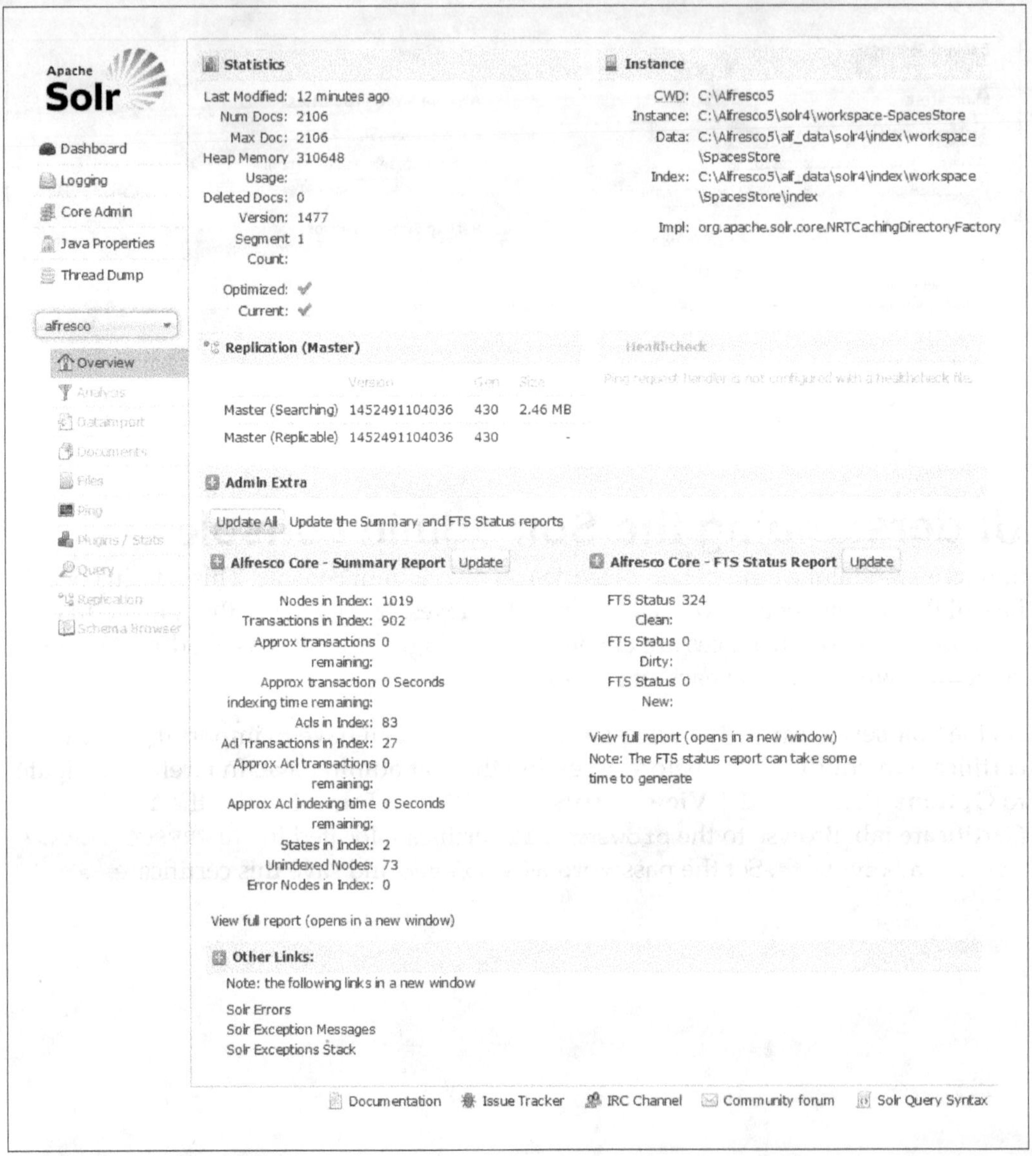
Apache Solr
Dashboard
Logging
Core Admin
Java Properties
Thread Dump
alfresco
Overview
Statistics
Last Modified: 12 minutes ago
Num Docs: 2106
Max Doc: 2106
Heap Memory Usage: 310648
Deleted Docs: 0
Version: 1477
Segment Count: 1
Optimized:
Current:
Instance
CWD: C:\Alfresco5
Instance: C:\Alfresco5\solr4\workspace-SpacesStore
Data: C:\Alfresco5\alf_data\solr4\index\workspace\SpacesStore
Index: C:\Alfresco5\alf_data\solr4\index\workspace\SpacesStore\index
Impl: org.apache.solr.core.NRTCachingDirectoryFactory
Replication (Master)
Master (Searching) 1452491104036 430 2.46 MB
Master (Replicable) 1452491104036 430 -
Admin Extra
Update All Update the Summary and FTS Status reports
Alfresco Core - Summary Report Update
Nodes in Index: 1019
Transactions in Index: 902
Approx transactions remaining: 0
Approx transaction indexing time remaining: 0 Seconds
Acls in Index: 83
Acl Transactions in Index: 27
Approx Acl transactions remaining: 0
Approx Acl indexing time remaining: 0 Seconds
States in Index: 2
Unindexed Nodes: 73
Error Nodes in Index: 0
View full report (opens in a new window)
Alfresco Core - FTS Status Report Update
FTS Status Clean: 324
FTS Status Dirty: 0
FTS Status New: 0
View full report (opens in a new window)
Note: The FTS status report can take some time to generate
Other Links:
Note: the following links in a new window
Solr Errors
Solr Exception Messages
Solr Exceptions Stack
Documentation
Issue Tracker
IRC Channel
Community forum
Solr Query Syntax

This dashboard shows you the full statistics of the indexes. As you can see in the preceding screenshot, it also shows you the index count for each of the cores. There is also a summary report and FTS status report. One more important section is **Replication**. If you set up a master and slave between multiple Solr nodes, this section will show you the health status of each of the nodes.

On the left-hand side panel, there are more sections beneath **Dashboard**:

- **Logging**: This fetches the logs from the server log file and displays them in your browser. You can also edit the log level for various classes.
- **Core Admin**: This is the administration panel for each of the cores in Solr. For Alfresco, we have defined two cores: `alfresco` and `archive`. It allows the admin user to rename cores, optimize indexes for each core, and add new cores. Refer to the following screenshot:

Apache
Solr
Dashboard
Logging
Core Admin
Java Properties
Thread Dump
Core Selector
Add Core
alfresco
archive
Unload
Rename
Swap
Reload
Optimize
Core
startTime:
21 minutes ago
instanceDir:
C:\Alfresco5\solr4\workspace-SpacesStore\
dataDir:
C:\Alfresco5\alf_data\solr4\index\workspace\SpacesStore\
Index
lastModified:
10 minutes ago
version:
1477
numDocs:
2106
maxDoc:
2106
deletedDocs:
-
optimized:
current:
directory:
org.apache.lucene.store.NRTCachingDirectory:NRTCachingDirectory(MMapDirectory@C:\Alfresco5\alf_data\solr4\index\workspace\SpacesStore\index lockFactory=NativeFSLockFactory@C:\Alfresco5\alf_data\solr4\index\workspace\SpacesStore\index; maxCacheMB=48.0 maxMergeSizeMB=4.0)
Documentation
Issue Tracker
IRC Channel
Community forum
Solr Query Syntax

- **Thread Dump**: This page allows you to take the thread dump of the Solr server for analysis.

- **Core Selector**: This is a dropdown, listing all the available cores. You can individually administrate each core in Solr. Here, we have two cores: `alfresco` and `archive`. Select `alfresco` and the **Overview** section will show you details about that core, as shown in the following screenshot. **Overview** is similar to **Dashboard**, but here, only details about the single core are provided:

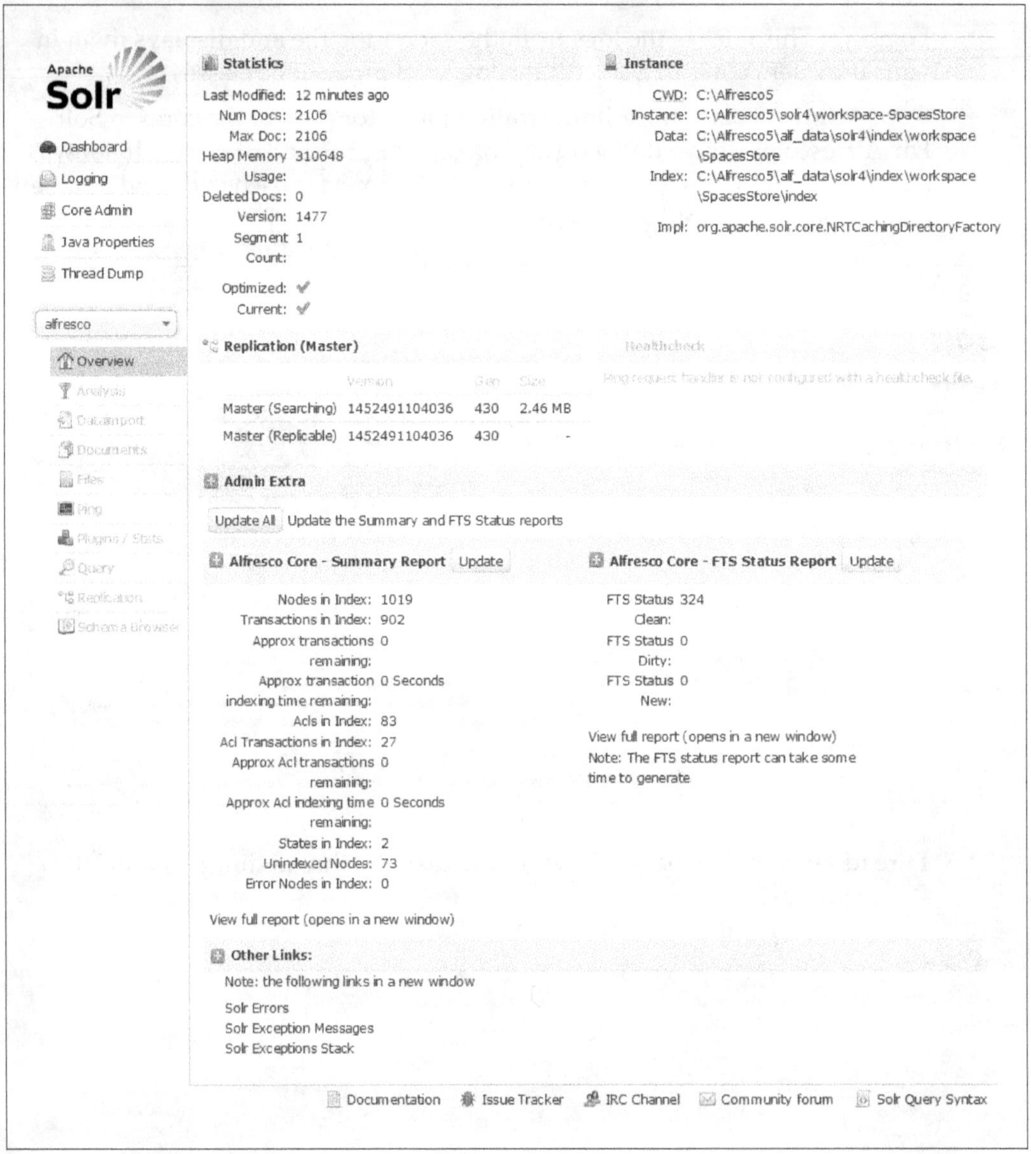
Apache Solr
Dashboard
Logging
Core Admin
Java Properties
Thread Dump
alfresco
Overview
Statistics
Last Modified: 12 minutes ago
Num Docs: 2106
Max Doc: 2106
Heap Memory Usage: 310648
Deleted Docs: 0
Version: 1477
Segment Count: 1
Optimized:
Current:
Instance
CWD: C:\Alfresco5
Instance: C:\Alfresco5\solr4\workspace-SpacesStore
Data: C:\Alfresco5\alf_data\solr4\index\workspace\SpacesStore
Index: C:\Alfresco5\alf_data\solr4\index\workspace\SpacesStore\index
Impl: org.apache.solr.core.NRTCachingDirectoryFactory
Replication (Master)
Master (Searching) 1452491104036 430 2.46 MB
Master (Replicable) 1452491104036 430 -
Admin Extra
Update All
Update the Summary and FTS Status reports
Alfresco Core - Summary Report
Update
Nodes in Index: 1019
Transactions in Index: 902
Approx transactions remaining: 0
Approx transaction indexing time remaining: 0 Seconds
Acls in Index: 83
Acl Transactions in Index: 27
Approx Acl transactions remaining: 0
Approx Acl indexing time remaining: 0 Seconds
States in Index: 2
Unindexed Nodes: 73
Error Nodes in Index: 0
View full report (opens in a new window)
Alfresco Core - FTS Status Report
Update
FTS Status Clean: 324
FTS Status Dirty: 0
FTS Status New: 0
View full report (opens in a new window)
Note: The FTS status report can take some time to generate
Other Links:
Note: the following links in a new window
Solr Errors
Solr Exception Messages
Solr Exceptions Stack
Documentation
Issue Tracker
IRC Channel
Community forum
Solr Query Syntax

Full re-indexing process in Solr

Full re-indexing in Solr is a very simple process. It cleans up all the current indexes, models, and content in Solr and restarts the application. Here are the steps in detail:

- Identify the index location from `solrcore.properties` for each of the cores. Generally, this file is located in <SOLR_HOME>/solr4/workspace-SpacesStore/conf and <SOLR_HOME>/solr4/archive-SpacesStore/conf
- The index location is set in property `data.dir.root`.
- Stop the Solr server.
- Remove indexes for both cores.
- Delete models and content in the same directory.
- Restart the Solr server.

Catching up the indexing process with the latest transactions can take time, depending on the repository size. If we clean up the indexes completely and restart, users won't be able to search until then. A better solution is to set up a new Solr instance, point it to the Alfresco server and start the crawling process. Once indexing is complete, re-point Alfresco to the new Solr server.

Troubleshooting Solr

Solr provides various Rest APIs to troubleshoot and re-index Solr Indexes. Here is a list of a few of them:

- Use the URL below to generate the health report of the Solr Indexes:
    - `https://localhost:8443/solr4/admin/cores?action=REPORT&wt=xml`

- This will generate a report about the health of each of the cores. This provides a count of total transactions, the last indexed transaction, and the commit time. If there are duplicate indexes it will show you the details, and if any transaction is not indexed, you can also identify that from this report. If your repository size is large, this report will take some time to generate. You can change the action to `Summary` to generate a summary report. Refer to the screenshot below for a detailed report:


```
- <lst name="report">
  - <lst name="alfresco">
      <str name="Alfresco version">5.0.0</str>
      <long name="DB acl transaction count">25</long>
      <long name="Count of duplicated acl transactions in the index">0</long>
      <long name="Count of acl transactions in the index but not the DB">2</long>
      <long name="First acl transaction in the index but not the DB">5</long>
      <long name="Count of missing acl transactions from the Index">0</long>
      <long name="Index acl transaction count">27</long>
      <long name="Index unique acl transaction count">27</long>
      <long name="Last indexed change set commit time">1434697644910</long>
      <str name="Last indexed change set commit date">2015-06-19T00:07:24</str>
      <long name="Last changeset id before holes">-1</long>
      <long name="DB transaction count">243</long>
      <long name="Count of duplicated transactions in the index">0</long>
      <long name="Count of transactions in the index but not the DB">56</long>
      <long name="First transaction in the index but not the DB">5</long>
      <long name="Count of missing transactions from the Index">0</long>
      <long name="Index transaction count">902</long>
      <long name="Index unique transaction count">902</long>
      <long name="Index node count">1019</long>
      <long name="Count of duplicate nodes in the index">4</long>
      <long name="First duplicate node id in the index">949</long>
      <long name="Index error count">0</long>
      <long name="Count of duplicate error docs in the index">0</long>
      <long name="Index unindexed count">73</long>
      <long name="Count of duplicate unindexed docs in the index">2</long>
      <long name="First duplicate unindexed in the index">959</long>
      <long name="Last indexed transaction commit time">1452490669570</long>
      <str name="Last indexed transaction commit date">2016-01-10T21:37:49</str>
      <long name="Last TX id before holes">-1</long>
      <long name="Node count with FTSStatus Clean">368</long>
      <long name="Node count with FTSStatus Dirty">0</long>
      <long name="Node count with FTSStatus New">0</long>
    </lst>
```


- Solr provides simple FIX action parameters to fix all the failed transactions or un-indexed nodes. By executing the URL below, it will verify all the transactions with the database and all the failed or un-indexed transactions will be fixed:
    - `https://localhost:8443/solr4/admin/cores?action=FIX`

- Administrators have the flexibility to delete or re-index a specific node, transaction or ACL ID in the repository. There are two action parameters available: `PURGE` to delete indexes and `RE-INDEX` to correct the indexes. Refer the following two sample URLs:
    - `https://localhost:8443/solr4/admin/cores?action=PURGE&txid=3675&acltxid=503&nodeid=8765&aclid=988`
    - `https://localhost:8443/solr4/admin/cores?action=REINDEX&txid=1563&acltxid=234&nodeid=9087&aclid=238`

Summary

In this chapter, we covered details about the search service in Alfresco. In Alfresco 5.x, searching is supported by the Solr4 search engine. There are various advantages to this new search engine: it is scalable, robust, conducts a fast search, and its performance is better. It polls Alfresco at certain intervals to track the new changes and re-index the data. Solr4 uses an asynchronous mode of indexing. You can also set up the replication of Solr servers via a master slave configuration. Solr4 provides its own admin console for administrators to monitor and troubleshoot the health of the server.

In the next chapter, we will cover details on permissions and roles in Alfresco. It will also provide details about integration with third party central authentication tools like LDAP.

6
Permissions and Security

In this chapter, we will discuss the permission and security model in Alfresco. The security model in Alfresco is flexible and allows you to choose the internal or external security model based on your organization setup via LDAP or the Active Directory system. You will also learn how to gain granular access control on content in the repository.

By the end of this chapter, you will have learned about:

- Understanding the security model
- The configuration of external security systems like LDAP and Active Directory
- Understanding permissions and roles

Overview of permissions and roles

The authorization of content in Alfresco is done by assigning users or groups (set of users) specific roles on folders or content. Roles are groups of permissions. There are a set of default roles available in Alfresco which we will learn about later in this chapter. There is also the flexibility to customize and define your new roles.

Users or groups can have specific permissions on spaces. Subspaces can inherit parent space permission. The Alfresco system is flexible enough that the subspaces and content can have specific permissions set without inheriting any of the parent space permissions.

Permissions

Access rights on any content or space can be defined in Alfresco by **permission**. Out of the box, there are multiple permissions. Any content in Alfresco is a node connected to other nodes using associations. By default, a space in Alfresco is a node (parent) that allows you to create instances of child associations for other nodes (children).

Any authority, like users or groups, can be granted any kind of permission on any node. Children of nodes inherit all the permissions from parents unless inheritance is explicitly set to off. When combining the permissions of parents and children, the highest permission takes precedence. The following are a few out of the box permissions:

- `ReadProperties`: This permission provides you control of access rights to read node metadata
- `ReadChildren`: This permission provides you control of access rights to fetch children of any node
- `ReadContent`: This permission is specific to content control if the user is allowed to read content
- `WriteProperties`: This permission provides you control of updating node metadata
- `WriteContent`: This permission provides you control of updating content.
- `DeleteNode`: This permission grants you the delete rights of content
- `DeleteChildren`: This permission grants you the delete rights of children of any node

All these permissions are defined in `permissionDefinitions.xml`, located at `<TOMCAT_HOME>/webapps/alfresco/WEB-INF/classes/alfresco/model`.

In the latest version since Alfresco v 5.0, these files have been moved inside the JAR file; `alfresco-repository-5.0.jar`.

Roles

Roles are a set of permissions. Out of the box, Alfresco supports five kinds of roles, listed as follows:

- `Consumer`: This role is with minimal permission. As the name suggests, it only grants `read` permissions to the user. Any user with the `Consumer` role on a folder or content can just read content, properties, and children. So, the `Consumer` role has three permissions grouped together: `ReadChildren`, `ReadContent`, and `ReadProperties`.

- `Editor`: This role has all the same rights as the `Consumer` role, plus `write` permission. A user with the `Editor` role can edit properties of nodes and edit the content of a node. `Editor` cannot upload new content.
- `Contributor`: As the name suggests, this role allows the user to upload content in space. `Contributor` becomes owner of the content uploaded by them and get full access rights to that content. So, `Contributor` can modify only the content uploaded by them. If you change the ownership of content, `Contributor` would not have any rights to edit the content. So, in short, the contributor is `Consumer` plus `AddChildren` permission.
- `Collaborator`: This role is a combination of `Editor` and `Contributor`. So, users with the `Collaborator` role can upload content and edit the content uploaded by others in that space.
- `Coordinator`: This role is the most powerful one. It grants the user full rights to the space. The user gets all the rights like an admin user on an assigned space. Be very careful when you grant this role to users. Users can modify permissions, delete nodes and children, upload content, create subspace, create rules, and so on.

All these permissions are defined in `permissionDefinitions.xml`, located at `<TOMCAT_HOME>/webapps/alfresco/WEB-INF/classes/alfresco/model`

In the latest version since Alfresco v 5.0, these files have been moved inside the JAR file `alfresco-repository-5.0.jar`.

The following is an extract of the XML configuration for the `Contributor` role, defined in the `permissionDefinitions.xml` file

```
<permissionGroup name="Contributor" allowFullControl="false"
  expose="true" >

    <includePermissionGroup permissionGroup="Consumer"
      type="cm:cmobject"/>
    <includePermissionGroup permissionGroup="AddChildren"
      type="sys:base"/>
    <includePermissionGroup permissionGroup="ReadPermissions"
      type="sys:base"/>

</permissionGroup>
```

If you want to create your custom role, you need to customize this `.xml` file. We are not covering this in detail as that is more of a development job.

Authorizing users the use of content or space

By now, you should know about the permissions and roles in Alfresco. In *Chapter 4, Administration of Alfresco*, we already learned about how users and groups are created. Once these users and groups are created in the repository, they need to be granted with specific access rights to spaces and content.

In most organizations, you have various departments and subsections within each department, as well as some people who belong to multiple departments.

For example, there are various teams like the HR team, recruitment team, management team, and administration team. Now, some people in the HR team would also be a part of the management team, and the recruitment team is a sub-set of the HR team. So, to organize such a hierarchy, you create various groups and subgroups.

Create a group in Alfresco named `HR_Team`, `Management_Team`, `Administration_Team`, as shown in *Chapter 4, Administration of Alfresco*. Now create a subgroup named `Recruitment_Team` under `HR_Team` as it is part of the `HR` group.

Create users and add them to the respective groups. Now your groups and users are ready. You need to assign permissions to groups in their respective folders so they have proper access.

Let's say that all users in the management team need permission on a folder named `Marketing`. Follow the steps below to grant access to the users:

1. Log in to Share using the URL, `http://<hostname:port>/share/`.
2. Select **Repository** in the top tool bar, which will take you to the **Document Library** page.
3. Navigate to the folder where you have to grant permission. For example, here `Marketing` is the root directory, as shown in following screenshot. Select the folder and in the **More...** menu, select **Manage Permission,** as shown in the following screenshot:

Marketing
Created just now by Administrator
No Description
No Tags
Favorite
Like 0
Comment
Shared (Shared Folder)
Created 44 minutes ago by System User
Folder to store shared stuff
No Tags
Favorite
Like 0
Comment
Download as Zip
View Details
Edit Properties
More...
Copy to...
Move to...
Manage Rules
Delete Folder
Manage Permissions
Manage Permissions

4. Now, in the manage permission page, you can edit the currently assigned permissions or invite new users or groups to the folder. Click the **Add User/ Group** button, search for the group or user you want to invite and click **Add**, as shown in following screenshots:

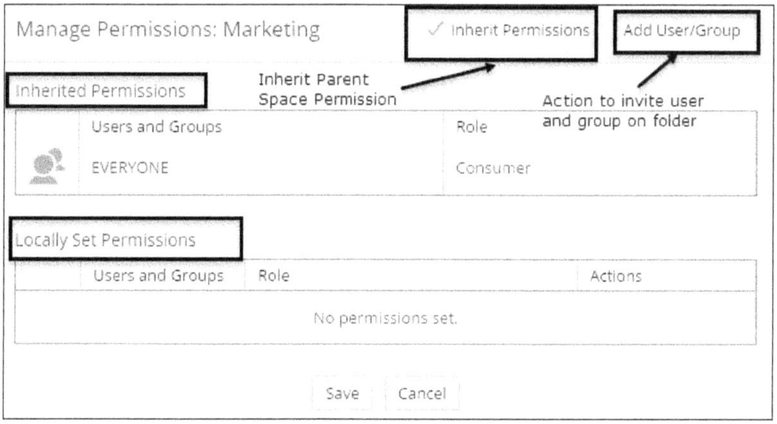
Manage Permissions: Marketing
Inherit Permissions
Add User/Group
Inherited Permissions
Inherit Parent Space Permission
Action to invite user and group on folder
Users and Groups
Role
EVERYONE
Consumer
Locally Set Permissions
Users and Groups
Role
Actions
No permissions set.
Save
Cancel

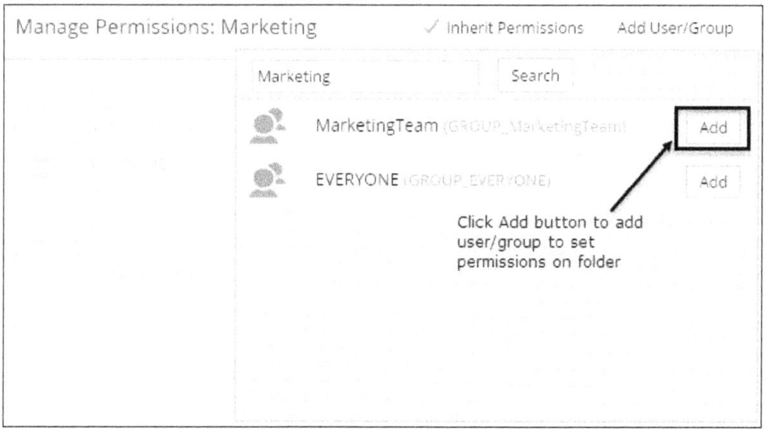
Manage Permissions: Marketing
Inherit Permissions
Add User/Group
Marketing
Search
MarketingTeam (GROUP_MarketingTeam)
Add
EVERYONE (GROUP_EVERYONE)
Add
Click Add button to add user/group to set permissions on folder

5. Now, this user/group will be listed in the **Locally Set Permissions** table.
6. Now change the role based on the kind of permission you want to grant that user/group by selecting the appropriate roles in the **Role** column.

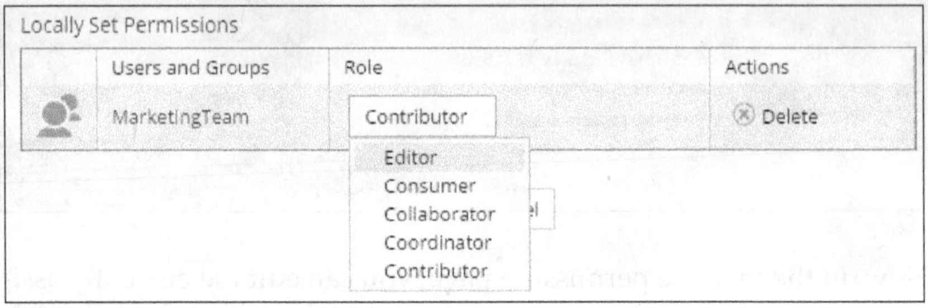

Locally Set Permissions
Users and Groups
Role
Actions
MarketingTeam
Contributor
Delete
Editor
Consumer
Collaborator
Coordinator
Contributor

7. At the top, there is a checkbox, **Inherit Permissions**, you can uncheck it if you don't want any parent folder permissions to be inherited by your folder. The **Inherited Permissions** table provides a list of permissions the selected folder has from the parent folder.
8. Click **Save** to save your changes.
9. If you want to remove any permissions from the folder, click the **Delete** button for the selected user/group, as shown in following screenshot, and click **Save**.

> In your folder hierarchy, if you are granting permission to a user at *nth* level from the root directory, make sure the user at least has `read` permissions on all the folders from the root directory to the *nth* level folder. Either keep the inheritance on or explicitly invite users/groups to all the folders. If permissions are not right in the complete tree, users will not be able to navigate properly or retrieve the documents which they have access to. Remember that you can set a role for specific content and if a user has the right role, he can access the content directly with the node reference without navigating the repository.

Overview of the security model

What we saw in earlier sections was that we have to create users and groups manually and then invite them to their respective folders. If you have thousands of users and you need to organize them in different groups based on your company policy, this would be a very long process.

Alfresco supports integration with external models like LDAP, AD, and so on. You can use this central authentication to manage users and groups in Alfresco. You can configure Alfresco to integrate with this centralized authentication security model and all the users and groups from this system would be synchronized in Alfresco.

For authentication, this external system would also be used, so user credentials are managed at a common location.

Alfresco also supports Single Sign On; you can log in into Alfresco with your machine credentials.

Authentication subsystem

The authentication subsystem includes the complete implementation of various security models. Here is the list of supported security models by Alfresco:

- `alfrescoNtlm`: This is the default authentication model where Alfresco user credentials would be stored in the Alfresco database
- `ldap`: As the name suggests, this is LDAP authentication using an external system like **OpenLDAP**
- `ldap-ad`: This refers to Active Directory authentication
- `kerberos`: This model is based on Kerberos authentication
- `passthru`: In this model, authentication is done via the Windows domain server or external servers
- `external`: This is an external authentication system

Authentication chain

Many organizations have multiple authentication servers. So, there are requirements where you need to integrate all the authentication systems with Alfresco. For that, the authentication subsystem provides the chaining mechanism. One instance of Alfresco can have more than one user source. However, the sequence in which these user data sources are chained is important. Considering the usage of the Alfresco database, an OpenLDAP server, and an AD server, when a user logs into the system, Alfresco checks for authentication in the sequence defined here:

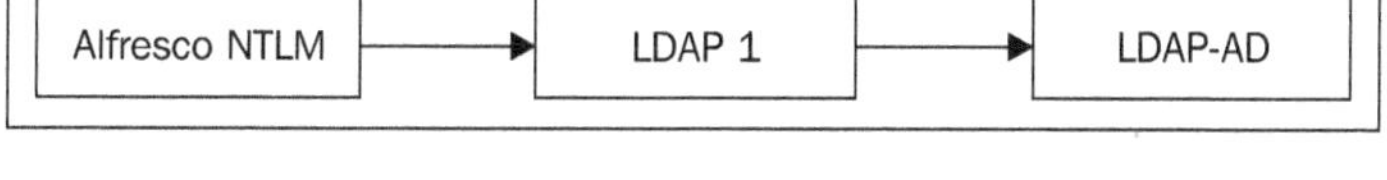
Alfresco NTLM
LDAP 1
LDAP-AD

The `authentication.chain` property defined in the `alfresco-global.properties` file specifies the authentication chain. The default authentication in chain is NTLM:

```
authentication.chain=alfrescoNtlm1:alfrescoNtlm < instance name : type
of authentication. It is same as like we create instance of any class
in Java>
```

Directory management in the Alfresco admin console shows the list of authentication chains and also allows you to configure and add new authentication models in the chain:

- `http://<ipaddress:port>/alfresco/s/enterprise/admin/admin-directorymanagement`

LDAP configuration with Active Directory

Let's say there is a marketing firm which uses Alfresco for managing their content, and all employees of the firm need to have access to Alfresco and use their common organization credentials which are stored in LDAP AD. This would require integration between Alfresco and LDAP AD. There are also a few external vendors who would need access to specific content in the Alfresco system, so instead of creating them in LDAP AD, they can be created internally within Alfresco. For this model, we would require Alfresco default authentication and LDAP AD integration.

With Alfresco 5.0, this whole process of adding a new authentication mechanism in a chain has become very easy. Now you can add any authentication, configure, test, and also synchronize all users and groups on the fly.

Follow the steps below to configure LDAP AD in an authentication chain:

1. Log in to the Alfresco admin console using the following URL; `http://<ipaddress:port>/alfresco/s/enterprise/admin/admin-directorymanagement`. This would land you at the **Directory Management** page. You should see a list of **Authentications** in the chain; by default, **alfrescoNtlm1** is already added in the chain.
2. In the **Authentication** chain section, provide an appropriate name for your LDAP connection and select the type of authentication as LDAP. Click **Add**. You need to click on **Save** and save the settings and after that, you should see the **Edit | Test** options. Refer to the following screenshot:

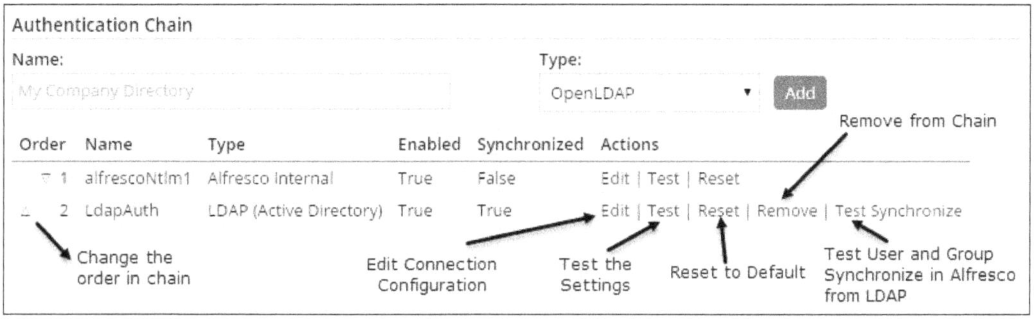
Authentication Chain
Name:
My Company Directory
Type:
OpenLDAP
Add
Remove from Chain
Order Name Type Enabled Synchronized Actions
1 alfrescoNtlm1 Alfresco Internal True False Edit | Test | Reset
2 LdapAuth LDAP (Active Directory) True True Edit | Test | Reset | Remove | Test Synchronize
Change the order in chain
Edit Connection Configuration
Test the Settings
Reset to Default
Test User and Group Synchronize in Alfresco from LDAP

3. Click on **Edit** to configure the LDAP settings to point to the correct server and provide synchronization details:
    - **Username format**: Map the user ID entered by the user to pass through LDAP; the `%s` is replaced with whatever the user types in as their user ID on the login screen
    - **LDAP server URL**: The name and port of your LDAP server; the standard port for LDAP is `389`
    - **Default administrator usernames**: The administrator user that connects to LDAP for authorization
    - **Security**: Security protocol used by server
    - **Synchronization enabled**: Enable this only if you want to synchronize the users and groups from LDAP
    - **Security principal name**: Principal account from which you can fetch user information from AD
    - **Security principal credentials**: Password for preceding principal account
    - **Group query**: LDAP query to fetch groups from LDAP
    - **Person query**: LDAP query to fetch persons from Active Directory
    - **User search base** : Specify the domain name from which you need to synchronize the users
4. Using the **Test** option, verify that LDAP configuration is correct.
5. There are few common settings required for the synchronization of users from LDAP which are under **Synchronization Settings**. This is common for all security models in a chain.

[The `import Cron` expression should be set to a time when the system load is reduced.]

6. If you want to manually trigger the sync process, click on the **Run Synchronize** button.

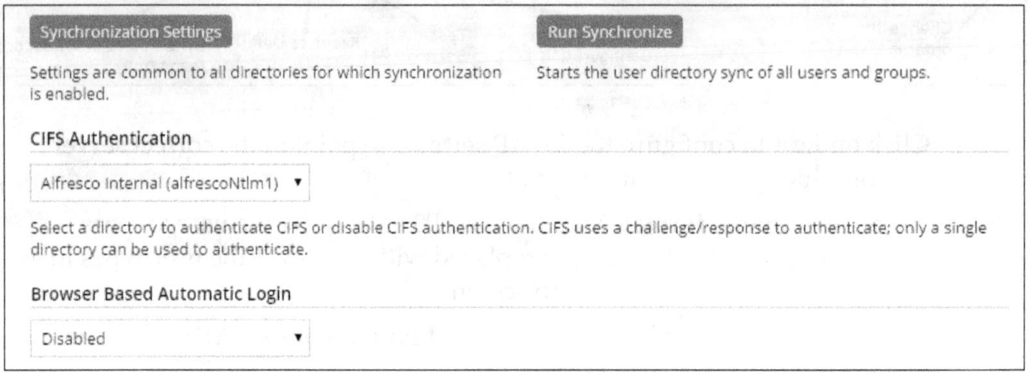
Synchronization Settings
Settings are common to all directories for which synchronization is enabled.
Run Synchronize
Starts the user directory sync of all users and groups.
CIFS Authentication
Alfresco Internal (alfrescoNtlm1)
Select a directory to authenticate CIFS or disable CIFS authentication. CIFS uses a challenge/response to authenticate; only a single directory can be used to authenticate.
Browser Based Automatic Login
Disabled

CIFS doesn't support LDAP AD configuration through an authentication chain. You need to configure `pass-thru` in an authentication chain. Edit the settings for `pass-thru`. The authentication server is an important property which needs to be configured as shown in the following screenshot.

Once `pass-thru` is configured, you can find it in the **CIFS Authentication** dropdown. Select the appropriate authentication and click **Save,** as shown in the following screenshot.

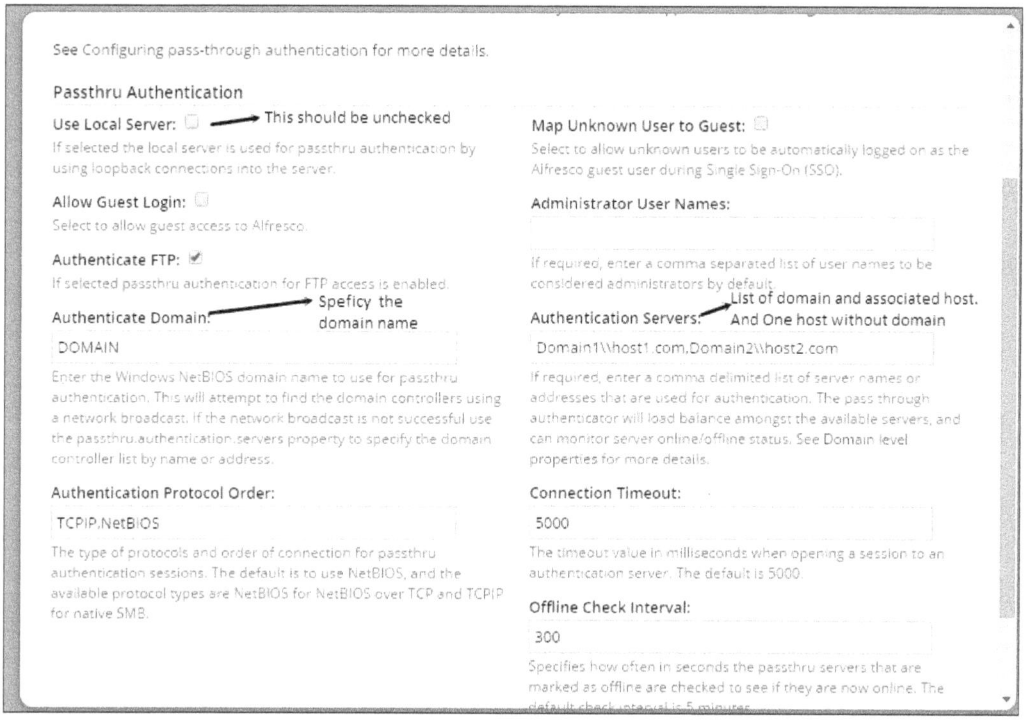
See Configuring pass-through authentication for more details.
Passthru Authentication
Use Local Server:
This should be unchecked
If selected the local server is used for passthru authentication by using loopback connections into the server.
Allow Guest Login:
Select to allow guest access to Alfresco.
Authenticate FTP:
If selected passthru authentication for FTP access is enabled.
Authenticate Domain:
Speficy the domain name
DOMAIN
Enter the Windows NetBIOS domain name to use for passthru authentication. This will attempt to find the domain controllers using a network broadcast. If the network broadcast is not successful use the passthru.authentication.servers property to specify the domain controller list by name or address.
Authentication Protocol Order:
TCPIP,NetBIOS
The type of protocols and order of connection for passthru authentication sessions. The default is to use NetBIOS, and the available protocol types are NetBIOS for NetBIOS over TCP and TCPIP for native SMB.
Map Unknown User to Guest:
Select to allow unknown users to be automatically logged on as the Alfresco guest user during Single Sign-On (SSO).
Administrator User Names:
If required, enter a comma separated list of user names to be considered administrators by default.
Authentication Servers:
List of domain and associated host. And One host without domain
Domain1\\host1.com,Domain2\\host2.com
If required, enter a comma delimited list of server names or addresses that are used for authentication. The pass through authenticator will load balance amongst the available servers, and can monitor server online/offline status. See Domain level properties for more details.
Connection Timeout:
5000
The timeout value in milliseconds when opening a session to an authentication server. The default is 5000.
Offline Check Interval:
300
Specifies how often in seconds the passthru servers that are marked as offline are checked to see if they are now online. The

Summary

Roles in Alfresco are groups of permissions. Users can be granted access rights to any content or folder by assigning them specific roles. There are various out of the box roles available in Alfresco like `Consumer`, `Contributor`, `Editor`, and `Coordinator`. You can also customize and create custom roles. Alfresco supports various security models like LDAP, Active Directory, and Kerberos to provide authentication from a centralized directory.

In the next chapter, we will discuss ways to cluster the Alfresco server for high availability.

7
High Availability in Alfresco

The high availability of any application is critical because of the global model of organizations. Also, with high throughput, multiple servers are required to support an application. This is where the clustering of nodes comes into the picture.

The typical requirements of high availability architectures are the following:

- Business continuity (up and running 24/7)
- Avoiding the single point of failure
- Hot backup
- Disaster recovery

In this chapter, we will discuss the ways of clustering in Alfresco and the backup restore process that supports the high availability of Alfresco.

By the end of this chapter, you will have learned about:

- Clustering Alfresco servers
- The backup process of Alfresco
- The restore process of Alfresco

Clustering Alfresco servers

Clustering refers to collections of multiple nodes combined together in a server as a single application to end users. With clustering, you can achieve scalability, server redundancy, and performance improvement of the application.

Let's consider a global financial organization that has multiple teams working for it across the globe. Alfresco is used as an enterprise content repository to store all the financial assets, like contracts. Now, these assets are very time-critical, and therefore the contracts should be accessible to all teams working on it at any time. There are thousands of users using the application, which also requires high server performance. High throughput is required for the server for users accessing assets in the system.

To satisfy these requirements, you will need to build a robust and highly available system by creating a clustered environment of Alfresco so the load on the server can be distributed. You also need a redundant and scalable environment so if one server goes down, you have another server up and running. This allows users to access the contracts from the application at any time. Moreover, you would have minimal downtime for the application.

There are various ways in which you can divide the servers in multiple tiers as per your requirements.

Replicating a complete stack

This approach is a straightforward approach where you create a replica of a complete stack and enable the clustering in Alfresco. The database and content store are being shared between all the nodes. Using a load balancer in front of this stack allows requests to be divided among servers. You can use any load balancer like Apache, Nginx, etc.

With this approach, if one node goes down, the other node is capable enough to serve the request independently.

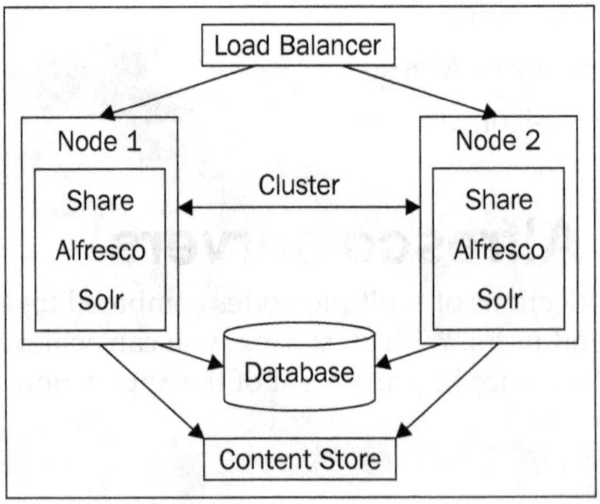
Load Balancer
Node 1
Share
Alfresco
Solr
Cluster
Node 2
Share
Alfresco
Solr
Database
Content Store

As the database and content store are shared among the servers, they are single points of failure. In addition to this, we have to manage the indexes in two Solr instances. For this, we would need a proper backup for the database and content store. More details on backup and restore will be covered later on in this chapter.

Multi-tier architecture

Each component of Alfresco can be divided into multiple tiers like Share, Repository, Database, and Solr. Use a load balancer to communicate between each tier. Share can either talk to the Alfresco Repository using the load balancer or an individual server. You can also have a common Solr server shared among all the nodes. Refer to the clustering diagram below for a visualization.

The database and content store are shared among the servers. This approach would be useful when you have to divide the load on the web-tier and increase the throughput of the application. In addition, indexes are available on the common Solr server, so there is no need to manage multiple instances. The Solr server can also be clustered together, which allows for easy scalability of the server.

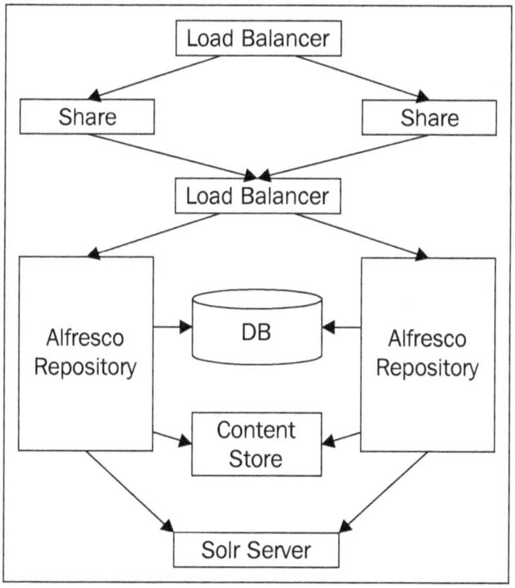
Load Balancer
Share
Share
Load Balancer
Alfresco Repository
DB
Alfresco Repository
Content Store
Solr Server

Clustering Alfresco nodes

Now we will understand the process required to cluster Alfresco nodes. As Share and Repository are different components, both require different configuration to bring them into the cluster.

First, identify what kind of clustering approach is required. Set up each node and make sure that each node as a single entity is working properly, such as being able to connect to the database and content store. Now follow the steps below to set up clustering between Alfresco nodes.

Step 1 – Share clustering

1. With Alfresco v 5.0, Hazelcast is used for clustering the web-tier nodes. Hazelcast sends multicast messaging between share node instances. Enable Hazelcast for Share.
2. Configure the `custom-slingshot-application-context.xml` file located at `<Tomcat_home>/shared/classes/alfresco/web-extension`. The sample file is already located in this location.
3. Rename the `.sample` file to a `.xml` file and uncomment the related Hazelcast configuration. Refer to the sample code with the book.
4. Configure the interface IP address based on your network.
5. Make sure that your Share instance communicates with Alfresco, which can either be via a load balancer or by hard-wiring the Alfresco instance in the Share configuration. If a load balancer is used then it should maintain a sticky session with the Alfresco instance.

Step 2 – repository clustering

1. Install and deploy Alfresco on multiple servers depending on the number of nodes you need.
2. Configure `alfresco-global.properties` located at `<Tomcat_home>/shared/classes/` on all nodes to point to the same database. Refer to *Chapter 3, Alfresco Configuration*, for configuring databases.
3. Make sure `dir.root` in the `alfresco-global.properties` file is pointing to same content store on all nodes. Mount the content store file system on all the nodes with the proper permission rights.
4. Set up the Solr instance and configure all Alfresco nodes to point to the common Solr instance.
5. Verify each node by starting them so that all configurations are correct, including Database, Solr, and Content Store. Once verified, stop the servers.

6. Now configure the clustering related properties below in the `alfresco-global.properties` file and restart all Alfresco nodes. Also make sure that the default clustering port `5701` is open on all nodes:
   - `alfresco.cluster.enabled=true`

     Set this value to `true` to enable clustering, if you set it to `false`, this node would not be part of clustering.
   - `alfresco.cluster.interface=10.208.*.*`

     This is the network interface to be used for clustering. You can define a wildcard value, so the system will try to bind with all interfaces having this IP address.
   - `alfresco.cluster.nodeType= Scheduler Server`

     Enter a human readable node name which helps to distinguish the servers. It is mostly useful for nodes which are not part of cluster, but which share the same database and content store.
   - `alfresco.hazelcast.password= clusterpasswd`

     Define the password used by clustered nodes to join or access the `hazelcast` cluster. From a security standpoint, always configure this property.
   - `alfresco.hazelcast.max.no.heartbeat.seconds=15`

     Configure the maximum node heartbeat timeout in seconds to assume it is dead.

Steps for verifying clustering

1. Verifying clustering with Alfresco v5.0 is very easy. Log in to the Alfresco Standalone Administration Page at `http://<server_name>:<port>/alfresco/service/enterprise/admin`.
2. Navigate to the **Repository Server** section and Click **Repository Server Clustering**. This page will provide you with the list of all cluster members. Click **Validate Cluster** to validate that all configurations are correct.

Another way to manually verify clustering is by uploading and searching content or a folder in the repository. Considering we have two Alfresco servers, `NODE1` and `NODE2`, in the clustered environment:

1. Log in to `NODE1` and upload some content.
2. Now log into `NODE2` and verify you are able to see the content.

3. Search for uploaded content in `NODE2` and verify you are able to search it.
4. Edit some metadata of the content or folder and verify that it has been updated on the other node.

Troubleshooting clustering

Enable debug logs for the class files listed below to troubleshoot in more detail. Make an entry in the `log4j.properties` file located at `<Tomcat_home>/webapps/alfresco/WEB-INF/classes` and restart the server:

- `log4j.logger.org.alfresco.enterprise.repo.cluster=info`

  This is the main package for clustering related classes.

- `log4j.logger.org.alfresco.enterprise.repo.cluster.core.ClusteringBootstrap=DEBUG`

  This provides detail about cluster startup, shutdown, whether it is disabled or if the license is invalid.

- `log4j.logger.org.alfresco.enterprise.repo.cluster.core.MembershipChangeLogger=DEBUG`

  This provides details about the cluster members.

- `log4j.logger.org.alfresco.enterprise.repo.cluster.cache=DEBUG`
- `log4j.logger.org.alfresco.repo.cache=DEBUG`

  This logs details about the cache of the server.

- `log4j.logger.com.hazelcast=info`

  Enable this if logging is required for core `hazelcast` packages.

Setting up the Hazelcast mancenter dashboard

The **Hazelcast mancenter** is a standalone application which allows you to monitor and manage all the servers using Hazelcast. This dashboard enables you to browse through the cluster data structure and provides you with details about the cluster. You can use this dashboard to get more details about the cluster node.

To set up this Hazelcast mancenter, follow these steps:

1. Install the Tomcat application server.
2. Download the Hazelcast mancenter WAR file and deploy in Tomcat.
3. Set up the data directory by adding the property below to the `CATALINA_OPTS` environment variable:

   ```
   -hazelcast.mancenter.home=/home/<tomcat_directory>/mancenter_data
   ```

4. Configure the Alfresco server to use this mancenter by adding the properties below in the `alfresco-global.properties` file. Make sure that from the Alfresco server, this mancenter service is accessible:

```
alfresco.hazelcast.mancenter.enabled=true
alfresco.hazelcast.mancenter.url=http://<tomcat-
erveraddress>:<port>/mancenter
```

> To get more details about the Hazelcast mancenter, refer to `http://hazelcast.com/products/management-center/`.

The backup and restore process

For an application to be robust, a proper backup process for all data is very important. Here, we will cover details about what steps are required for backing up and restoring data in Alfresco.

Backups are required for the main critical components of Alfresco which hold the data, as listed below.

- **Database**: You can use the database dump method based on the type of database used for backup. There is a very good tool, **Xtrabackup** for MySQL, using which, backing up a large database is trivial. Refer to `http://www.percona.com/software/percona-xtrabackup`. As the repository size grows, the DB size will be large, so an efficient and incremental backup and restore strategy should be defined for the database.
- **ContentStore (All Binary Files)**: Standard file system replication can be used to back up the content store. An important point to note here is that as your repository size grows, a full backup of the content store will become a time consuming process. So, always plan for an incremental backup. The frequency of content store backup is also very important as it will use network bandwidth.
- **Solr Indexes**: Alfresco provides a backup scheduler to back up Solr indexes. Perform a nightly backup for Solr indexes. You can define the backup time for Solr indexes using the Alfresco admin console. Details about this can be found in *Chapter 5, Search*.
- **Alfresco Configuration**: All installations and important configuration files should also be backed up in regular intervals. So if the system crashes, it will be very easy to set up the system again.

There are two methodologies of the backup process: cold and hot backup. Let's understand the process details of each of them.

Performing a cold backup

As the name suggests, with this approach we need to stop the Alfresco server and back up all the required components.

1. Stop the Alfresco Server.
2. Stop the Solr Server if it is not installed within Alfresco server.
3. Simultaneously, back up Solr Indexes, the content store and database. For Solr Indexes and the content store, use a standard file system backup process like **rsync**. For the database, use the standard database supported backup mechanism.
4. Store this backup in the same place as a single package.

This approach will provide you with a clean backup but the problem is, it would require the lengthy downtime of servers based on the repository size. It should only be done when you have planned server maintenance. This is not the recommended approach for regular backups.

Performing a hot backup

Here, backups are taken without stopping servers. Now, as you are taking a live backup of data, the backup order below needs to be followed.

- Solr Indexes backup
- Database backup
- Content store backup

The reason for this sequence is to make sure that database integrity is maintained with the content store. If you take the content store backup first, you have references to content in the database which are not present in the content store.

For taking a live backup of Solr and the content store, you can use a standard filesystem backup like rsync. Schedule a cron job in the operating system to backup these files at regular intervals. Solr Indexes backup is also taken care of by Alfresco by configuring the Solr backup properties in the Alfresco admin console.

In the case of databases, you can set up a master-slave for data replication. All the data from the master would be replicated to the slave. The slave would need the same amount of space as the master. You can also take the database dump at regular intervals, but make sure the dump procedure you use doesn't lock the database.

In addition to this, also take regular backups of the database at certain intervals, such as nightly, for handling scenarios where users may delete nodes from the system by mistake. With master-slave, if something is deleted in the master, it will also be propagated to the slave. Backing up the database at certain intervals allows you to go back to old copies in case it is required.

It is recommended to have a strong, well-thought-out backup strategy already defined when you install the Alfresco application. Incremental backup at regular intervals is a feasible method for big repositories, but at some point, as part of maintenance, take a full backup of system.

The restore process

Take the latest backup copy of all three components (Database, Solr indexes, Content store). All components should be from the same backup unit.

1. Stop the Alfresco server.
2. Restore the database from backup. Configure `alfresco-global.properties` to point to the new restored database. Restoring the database will be based on the backup strategy used and database vendor.
3. Copy Solr Indexes from backup. Make sure the `data.dir.root` property in `solrcore.properties` is pointing to the new index folder. In Alfresco, there are different Solr configuration files for the workspace and archive store, so you have to restore both indexes in their respective directories.
4. Restore the Content Store and modify `dir.root` in `alfresco-global.properties` to point to the new restored content store.
5. Restart the Alfresco server. Log in and verify that the restore worked properly.

Designing a disaster recovery system for Alfresco

Disaster recovery is required for business continuity with the minimum application downtime. For any critical application, the downtime of servers can be a big loss to business. So, it is very important to set up disaster recovery servers. These servers should be in a different location to where your production servers are.

For disaster recovery in Alfresco, you need to set up the complete Alfresco stack at a different data center location. This secondary system will be on read only mode or it will not be in a running state. This disaster recovery setup is different to the clustering process.

For setting up the disaster recovery of the Alfresco application, follow the steps below.

1. Set up your application in a similar fashion to that of your production server. Use the same hardware and same application stack.
2. This new disaster recovery server will not be in cluster mode with the production server.
3. Now you need to set up replication for the database, content store, indexes, and application configuration. Try to find the optimal replication plan based on your repository size, growth rate, and read and write operations.
4. All of the components should be replicated on a regular basis so you can recover data as close to production as possible. Here, an important point to be considered is your network bandwidth and latency. As the servers will be geographically scattered apart, network latency will become more important.
5. In case of production failure, turn on the DR server and configure it in production. Configure the load balancer to redirect the request to a new server. With this, you can get the servers up and running in minimal downtime. Users can still use the application by the time you have recovered the system.

Here is a diagram of how your typical DR structure would be:

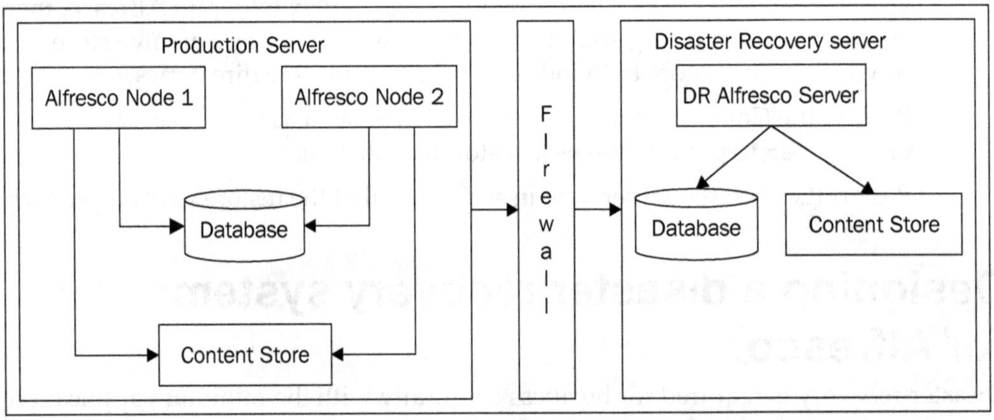
Production Server
Alfresco Node 1
Alfresco Node 2
Database
Content Store
Firewall
Disaster Recovery server
DR Alfresco Server
Database
Content Store

Summary

The Alfresco server can be clustered together to have a more robust, scalable, and highly available ECM server. Alfresco provides you with the flexibility to distribute the nodes and cluster them in multiple tiers based on your requirements. Repository and Share clustering is supported by Hazelcast. The Admin Console of Alfresco provides you with details about all the clustered nodes and also allows admin users to verify the clustering of nodes. Alfresco doesn't provide its own backup and restore process, but we can use industry-standard filesystem and database backup mechanisms to ensure a robust backup of your applications.

In the next chapter, we will talk about how Alfresco actually stores content. The content lifecycle will also be discussed in detail. This chapter will also cover in detail the important tables in the Alfresco database.

8
The Basics of the Alfresco Content Store

Content is the heart of the ECM system. All functionalities and features of the ECM system are surrounded by content. For the architecture and maintenance of the ECM system, the understanding of the lifecycle of content in an ECM application is very important. Once content gets inside the CMS application, it passes through different phases, which is common in most standard ECM applications.

However, the storage mechanism of the content varies in different ECM applications.

In this chapter, we will understand, in detail, the lifecycle of content in Alfresco and how these different phases impact different components of Alfresco. We will also try to understand the Alfresco database schema.

By the end of this chapter, you will have learned about:

- The content lifecycle
- Content store types
- Alfresco database schema

Before going into detail about lifecycles, let's understand the content store and database schema. We already covered indexes in *Chapter 5, Search*.

Understanding the content store architecture

The content store controls the creation and deletion of binary content in the filesystem. We have already covered a few details on this in earlier chapters. The `dir.root` property in the `alfresco-global.properties` (`<Tomcat_Home>/shared/classes`) file defines the root binary file storage location.

Let's, for example, examine the path specified in `dir.root` which is `/mnt/alf_data`. Beneath this directory, there are two folders: `contentstore` and `contentstore.deleted`, which will be created the first time Alfresco is started. Let's have a look at the details of the folder:

- `contentstore`: All active and archive content is being stored here. Based on content creation time, a directory hierarchy is created. All the files will have a unique name and the `.bin` extension. Let's say there is a file named `Employee Handbook.doc` being uploaded in Alfresco on January 20, 2015 at 10:50 A.M., then the file will be stored in `/mnt/alf_data/contentstore/2015/1/20/10/50/<unique name>.bin`.
- `contentstore.deleted`: The orphaned content which is permanently deleted by Alfresco is being moved to this directory by an orphan cleaner scheduler. From this directory, files can be removed at any time using the standard operating system remove command. For example, by executing the `rm /mnt/alf_data/contentstore.deleted/2015/1/23/13/34/xxxxx.bin` command.

This is the general architecture of a default content store. The default content store is named `FileContentStore`. Based on this default content store, Alfresco also provides various different types of content store. Here are a few details about each type of content store.

Encrypted ContentStore

As the name suggests, the content is stored encrypted in the filesystem. All content is encrypted with its unique key. This unique key is again encrypted with a master key and is stored in the Alfresco database. The encrypted ContentStore was introduced in version 5.0 of Alfresco . To enable the encrypted ContentStore, you will need a license file, which has enabled content store encryption from Alfresco.

Enabling the encrypted ContentStore

Here are the steps required to enable and configure the encrypted ContentStore.

1. Get the license file with encrypted ContentStore enabled. Install the new license file using the admin console. Refer to *Chapter 4, Administration of Alfresco.*
2. An RSA key needs to be generated in a new `keystore` using `keytool`. A sample `keytool` command can be used to generate the master key.

   ```
   keytool -genkey -alias key1 -keyalg RSA -keystore <master
   keystore path> -keysize 2048
   ```

3. Configure the following properties in `alfresco-global.properties` to enable content encryption. These properties can also be changed via JMX:
   - `filecontentstore.subsystem.name=encryptedContentStore`

     This will enable the encrypted content store
   - `cryptodoc.jce.keystore.type=`

     This is the `keystore` type for master keys like `jceks`
   - `cryptodoc.jce.keystore.path=`

     Provides the path of the `keystore` where the master key was generated
   - `cryptodoc.jce.keystore.password=`

     Password for `keystore`
   - `cryptodoc.jce.key.aliases=`

     A comma separated list of all aliases of the master key
   - `cryptodoc.jce.key.passwords=`

     A comma separated list of all passwords for fetching the master key from the `keystore`
   - `cryptodoc.jce.keygen.defaultSymmetricKeySize=`

     The size of the symmetric key size by default is 128 bit
4. The `dir.root` path specified in `alfresco-global.properties` remains the same.

> Once enabled, you cannot revert back to the normal ContentStore. Also, if you are upgrading from an old version, only new content will be encrypted. Old content will still remain un-encrypted. Be careful when you choose the encrypted ContentStore. Multi-tenancy is not supported with an encrypted store.

Caching ContentStore

Caching ContentStore works as a wrapper around any ContentStore to provide caching and faster access of data. Caching ContentStore should be used with either a slow disk, Amazon s3, or so on. If the normal content storage mechanism is slow, set up the caching ContentStore around it. Don't use it around FileContentStore if you have a fast disk.

Configuring the caching of ContentStore

Follow the steps below to configure the caching of ContentStore (assuming the backing store is already configured).

1. Enable the caching-content-store-context.xml file located at <ALFRESCO_HOME>/shared/classes/alfresco/extension by renaming it from .sample to .xml.
2. Configure the context file as per your system requirements. Refer to the bean ID cachingContentStore. Make sure the backingStore and quota are configured properly. Quota can be standard quota or unlimited. With a standard quota manager, you can control the disk usage of cached files:

```
<bean id="cachingContentStore"
class="org.alfresco.repo.content.caching.CachingContentStore"
init-method="init">
    <property name="backingStore" ref="backingStore"/>
    <property name="cache" ref="contentCache"/>
    <property name="cacheOnInbound"
      value="${system.content.caching.cacheOnInbound}"/>
    <property name="quota" ref="standardQuotaManager"/>
</bean>
```

3. In the sample context file, the `backingStore` bean is referring to `FileContentStore`. Change the bean definition based on the backing store used. With `FileContentStore`, there is no use of caching. For example, if you are using `S3ContentStore` (details about this content store will be covered later on in this chapter) where caching is required, make sure the `backingStore` is referring to the correct `ContentStore`, as shown in the following sample code snippet:

```
<bean id="backingStore"
class="org.alfresco.integrations.s3store.TenantS3ContentStore">
    <constructor-arg>
        <value>${dir.contentstore}</value>
    </constructor-arg>
</bean>
```

4. Based on the context file configuration, add and modify the following important properties in the `alfresco-global.properties` file. Default values are set in the `repostiory.properties` file:
   - `dir.cachedcontent=${dir.root}/cachedcontent:`

     Change this value if you want the cached content in a different path to the content root directory.
   - `system.content.caching.cacheOnInbound=true`

     This is the property to enable the caching of content while running the write operation. That way, whenever content is read, it is already in the cache.
   - `system.content.caching.maxDeleteWatchCount=1:`

     The number of times the file is observed as deleted before cleanup from the cache.
   - `system.content.caching.contentCleanup.cronExpression=0 0 3`

     Specify the cron expression to clean up the cached content.
   - `system.content.caching.minFileAgeMillis=60000`

     Specify the minimum live time for the file before it is deleted from the cache.
   - `system.content.caching.maxUsageMB=4096`

     This property is associated with a quota, the maximum amount of disk space can be used for the cache.
   - `system.content.caching.maxFileSizeMB=0`

     Change this value if you want any limitations with the file size to be maintained in the cache.

Alfresco S3 content store

This is a special content store which will be required only when the Alfresco instance is on the Amazon cloud (EC2) (refer to `https://en.wikipedia.org/wiki/Amazon_Web_Services` for more details). Alfresco provides this additional module to use **Amazon's Simple Storage Service (S3)** for file storage. The **Alfresco S3** content store is slower than the standard `FileContentStore`, so you can use this in combination with the caching ContentStore.

Configuring the Alfresco S3 connector

Follow these steps to configure the S3 connector:

1. Download the `amp` package for the S3 connector from Alfresco support.
2. Install this `amp` package using the **Alfresco Module Package** (**AMP**) installation procedure.
3. Configure the following properties in the `alfresco-global.properties` file
    - `s3.accessKey=`

      Specify the access key for Amazon Web service identification.
    - `s3.secretKey=`

      Specify the Amazon web service secret key.
    - `s3.bucketName=`

      Specify the bucket name which will be used for content storage. This bucket name should be unique.
4. Once the bucket name is defined, the same bucket can be used to multipurpose. Define the `contentstore` and `contentstore.deleted` paths using the same bucket name in the `alfresco-global.properties` file.

```
dir.contentstore=/AmazonBucketPath/contentstore
dir.contentstore.deleted=/AmazonBucketPath/contentstore.deleted
```

[When upgrading from the local content store to S3, the content store will not be supported by S3. It will corrupt the repository.]

Content store selector

The content store selector provides users with a mechanism to bind content with a specific content store. Alfresco provides the flexibility to have multiple content stores, and you can decide what content needs to be stored in which store. This is very useful in a scenario where you need to store different folder data in a completely different store. You get the flexibility to place the less read, old content to any slow disk and all new content to any fast disk.

Using the content store selector

Follow the steps mentioned here to enable the content store selector:

1. Create a content store selector context file in `<Alfresco_home>/shared/classes/alfresco/extension`. A sample context file is provided with support files of this book.
2. Define the store as you require by defining beans, as shown in the following code sample:

```
<bean id="projectMarketingContentStore" class="org.alfresco.repo.
content.filestore.FileContentStore">
    <constructor-arg>
        <value>${dir.root}/storeProjectA</value>
    </constructor-arg>
</bean>
```

3. List all the store beans with a store name that will be visible in the user interface in the `storeSelectorContentStore` bean. Take a look at the sample code snippet:

```
<bean id="storeSelectorContentStore" parent="storeSelectorContentS
toreBase">
   <property name="defaultStoreName">
      <value>default</value>
   </property>
   <property name="storesByName">
      <map>
          <entry key="default">
             <ref bean="fileContentStore" />
          </entry>
          <entry key="projectMarketing">
             <ref bean="projectMarketingContentStore " />
          </entry>
            ...
   <bean>
```

4. Configure the `eagerOrphanCleanup` bean to map this list, so all this additional content store can be cleaned up in the same fashion as the default content store.
5. Set a proper scheduler cron expression for the `system.content.orphanCleanup.cronExpression` property in `alfresco-global.properties`.
6. Now restart Alfresco.
7. For Share, you need to enable the `cm:storeSelector` aspect and `cm:storeName`, which is a property associated with this aspect.

   Find the `aspects` tag in the `share-config-custom.xml` file located at `<ALFRESCO_HOME>/tomcat/shared/classes/alfresco/web-extension` and below the `storeSelector` aspect, add it in the list as shown in the following code snippet:

   ```
   <aspects>
       <!-- Aspects that a user can see -->
           <visible>
               ..
               <aspect name="cm:storeSelector" />
            </visible>
               ..
   </aspects>
   ```

   Also define the user-friendly name of the aspect in the `slingshot.properties` file to be shown in the Share user interface.

   ```
   aspect.cm_storeSelector=Store Selector
   ```

8. Now apply this aspect to any content and set the `storeName` based on the store you want the content to be in, for example if you want to store all marketing documents in the `projectMarketing` store, set the `storeName` value to `projectMarketing` as defined in the store selector bean. The file will be copied from the default content store to the new content store. If no value is specified in `storeName`, it takes the default. The file in the old content store will remain as it is, but it will be marked as orphan so the cleanup process can clean these documents.

Understanding the database schema

Alfresco has its own standard database schema to store all its information. The database is the heart of the whole CMS system.

External applications, apart from Alfresco, should not perform any write operations in the Alfresco database directly. Always make sure you use the database for reading only. This is a standard practice. Don't make any changes to any values in the database. This schema is only required to understand Alfresco and troubleshoot.

As you know, everything in Alfresco is based around nodes, so the tables are also named in the same pattern. The database schema of Alfresco is very easy to understand. So, here we will not dive into all the tables, only a few important ones will be covered.

Schema of the alf_node table

This table is the main primary reference of the node. This is the first table you will always look for. All the node entries are present in this table. It captures primary node information like UUID, created date, modified date, creator, transaction ID , permission information, and so on. Here are the details about some of the columns of this table.

- `id`: This is the unique database ID for each node in Alfresco. This same ID is being referenced in other tables.
- `store_id`: This ID refers to the unique ID from the `alf_store` table. This ID signifies which store this node belongs to, like `workspacesStore`, `archivespacesStore`, or `usersStore`, and so on.
- `uuid`: This is the unique node ID which is used in all the services and interfaces that refer to this node. This UUID never changes for a node as long as a node is present in the Alfresco system.
- `transaction_id`: This refers to the ID column in the `alf_transaction` table. Any `write` operation in Alfresco is considered to be processed within a transaction. Every node is part of a transaction. If you do a batch operation, there is a possibility that all nodes will have the same transaction ID. While indexing in Alfresco, based on these transaction IDs, all nodes are fetched from the database and indexed in Solr. So, this transaction ID is also a very important column.
- `type_qname_id`: This column is the foreign key reference ID from the `alf_qname` table. It defines the type of node like content, folder, person, and so on.

- `acl_id`: This ID refers to the unique ID in the `alf_access_control_list` table related to permission. Permission in Alfresco can be considered a map; all this information is stored in a different table structure. `acl_id` will lead to all permissions available on this node.
- `auditor_creator`: This column captures information about the user who created this node.
- `auditor_created`: This column captures the time this node was created in the system.
- `auditor_modified`: This column captures the time this node was modified.

Schema of the alf_node_properties table

This is another important table. As the name suggests, this table stores metadata information about the node like its name, description, and content store path ID. All the node references are stored in this table. This table could be a giant table; if you have five properties for a node, there would be five rows in this table. As all the information is tied to a unique node ID, it is very easy to fetch information from the table.

Here is the list of a few important columns in this table:

- `node_id`: This column refers to the unique database ID of the node defined in the `alf_node` table.
- `actual_type_n`: This column defines the property type.
- `boolean_value`: This column stores the values of any Boolean value metadata of node.
- `string_value`: This column stores the values of any string valued metadata of the node.
- `long_value`: If the metadata value is referring to some other table, the ID of that table will be in this column. For example, the binary file location of an asset is captured in different tables. The ID referring to that entry is stored in this column.
- `qname_id`: This column stores the namespace and property name referring to its ID in the `alf_qname` table.

Schema of the alf_child_assoc table

This table stores all the parent-child association or peer-to-peer association information. With this table, you can identify the child and parent of any node.

- `parent_node_id`: This column stores the unique node database ID referring to the ID column of the `alf_node` table. As the name suggests, this would represent the parent node ID.
- `child_node_id`: This column stores the unique node database ID referring to the ID column of the `alf_node` table. This provides the node information of the child under the associated parent node ID.
- `child_node_name`: This column stores the names of the children nodes.
- `type_qname_id`: This column specifies the type of the node.
- `qname_ns_id`: This column refers to the ID column of the `alf_namespace` table.

Schema of the alf_content_data table

This table stores the mapping of node and binary file location. All the required information related to binary content is stored in this table. Here is the information about each of the columns:

- `id`: This column stores the unique row ID; this ID is being used to map the node and binary content. The `alf_node_properties` file defining the `cm:content` property will have this unique ID.
- `content_url_id`: This refers to the ID in the `alf_content_url` table. This ID will lead to the actual path of content in the filesystem.
- `content_mimetype_id`: This column specifies the mime-type of the content, which will be required for `read-write` operations on content.
- `content_encoding_id`: This column specifies the encoding of content.

Schema of the alf_content_url table

This table has the actual filesytem path information about the binary file. Here is the information about each of the columns:

- `id`: This column stores the unique row ID. This same ID is a reference point to fetch the URL information.
- `content_url`: This contains the actual filesystem location of the binary file under the `contentstore` directory. A sample entry would be `store://2015/2/10/20/30/xxxx-xxxx-xxx.bin`.

- `content_size`: This stores the specified size of the content.
- `orphan_time`: This column is very important. When content is permanently deleted from the Alfresco system, this column will have orphan time. Based on this time, the cleanup process cleans up all the orphaned content from the filesystem.

> Don't try to change values in a database directly unless you are certain about the consequences. Even though you have to make changes, always have a backup and rollback plan in place.

Understanding the content lifecycle in Alfresco

All content in Alfresco has a lifecycle in its system. There are mainly two stages in which content could be in any ECM system. Here are the following stages:

- **Live state** : It is referred to as `workSpacesStore` in Alfresco
- **Archive state**: It is referred to as `archiveSpacesStore` in Alfresco

When a user uploads content, it is in a live state. Users can do all sorts of operations like edit, update, and change permissions while content is in an active state. On deletion of content, users have the option to send the content to an archive state, and keep it there for a specific duration and then have it removed completely from the system or permanently deleted from Alfresco.

As we discussed in earlier chapters, Alfresco has three components: **Database**, **ContentStore**, and **Solr Indexes,** which keep reference to all of the content within the system. So, the content lifecycle mainly impacts these three components.

Let's go through, in detail, the content lifecycle and the impact of each action to these components.

Creating content

On creation of content in Alfresco, it is stored in a live store, which is `workSpacesStore`. All content has a binary file and its associated metadata. Metadata and all its references are stored in Database. The binary file is stored in ContentStore. For Search, all the required indexes are created in the `Solr` directory:

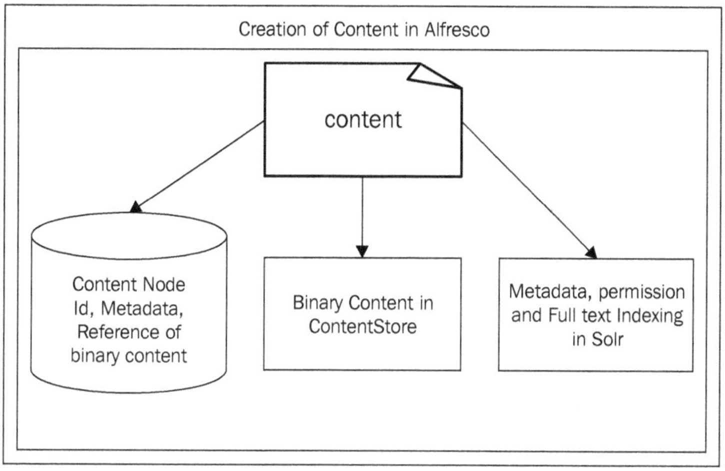
Creation of Content in Alfresco
content
Content Node Id, Metadata, Reference of binary content
Binary Content in ContentStore
Metadata, permission and Full text Indexing in Solr

Editing content

Editing content in Alfresco could either mean editing the actual data of a document or its associated metadata. If a user updates the content of Alfresco, a new binary file is created in ContentStore and a reference to it is updated in Database. The old binary file is marked as an orphan for removal from the system. Details about the orphan lifecycle will be explained later on in the chapter. Solr indexes are also updated if the content requires full indexing.

If only the metadata of a document is updated, the associated entry in the database is modified. Also, old indexes are removed and new Solr indexes are created for the updated metadata:

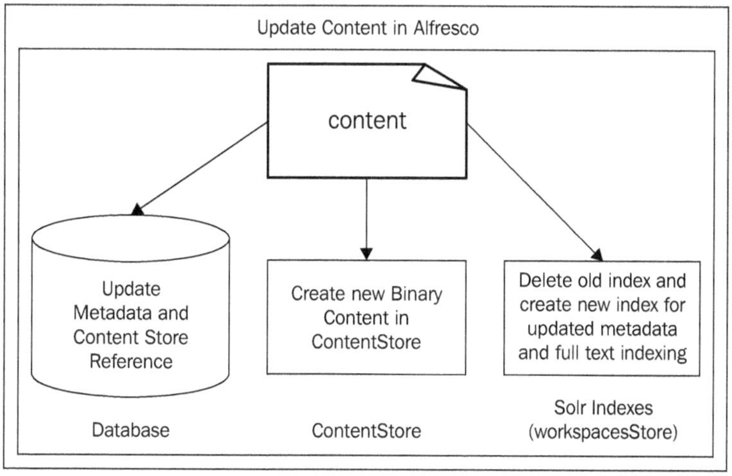
Update Content in Alfresco
content
Update Metadata and Content Store Reference
Create new Binary Content in ContentStore
Delete old index and create new index for updated metadata and full text indexing
Database
ContentStore
Solr Indexes (workspacesStore)

Archiving content

When a user deletes content from the live store, it is moved to the archive store. In Alfresco, you can view all the archive content in the trash can. When content is archived, the main reference table (`alf_node`) has new entries related to the archive store. A new archive node ID is generated for the document and all metadata references to it are associated with this new node ID. The old node ID is marked as deleted. There is no impact to the binary file in ContentStore. Indexes are removed from `workspaceStore` and created under `archivespaceStore`:

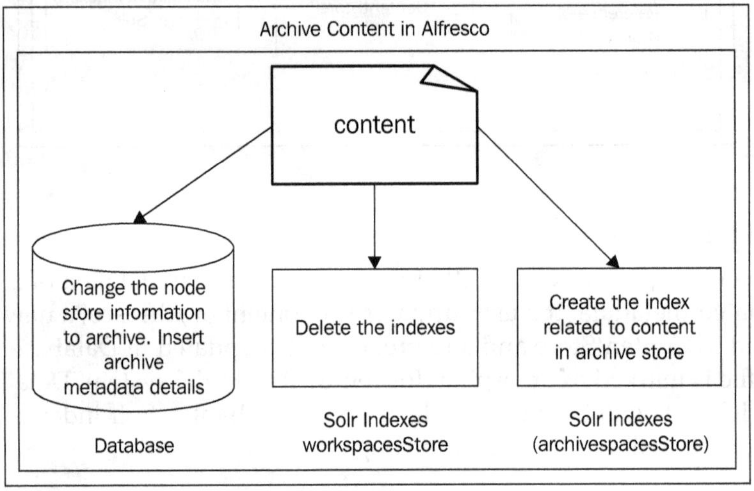
Archive Content in Alfresco
content
Change the node store information to archive. Insert archive metadata details
Database
Delete the indexes
Solr Indexes workspacesStore
Create the index related to content in archive store
Solr Indexes (archivespacesStore)

Deleting content

This is the phase when a user wants to delete the file from the system permanently. When a user removes content from the trash can, content is permanently marked for deletion. There is no rollback at this point. All metadata information is removed from the database. Only one entry is present in the main reference table (`alf_node`), which is marked for deletion. After 30 days, the entry from the database will also be removed. The binary file is not marked for deletion immediately, but the content location mapping in the database is marked as an orphan. After 14 days, the binary file will be moved to the `contentstore.deleted` directory in the filesystem. The amount of ContentStore protection in days is configurable. All the indexes are removed completely when the file is deleted permanently:

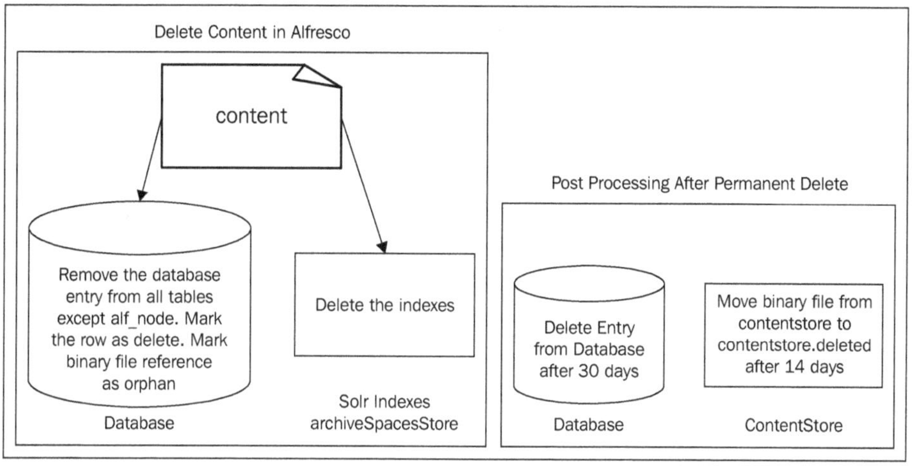
Delete Content in Alfresco
content
Remove the database entry from all tables except alf_node. Mark the row as delete. Mark binary file reference as orphan
Database
Delete the indexes
Solr Indexes archiveSpacesStore
Post Processing After Permanent Delete
Delete Entry from Database after 30 days
Database
Move binary file from contentstore to contentstore.deleted after 14 days
ContentStore

In Alfresco, everything is considered a node. What we have learned above about the content lifecycle is mostly applicable to all types of nodes. But apart from content, we also have folders, users, and groups in Alfresco. These special types of nodes have some differences when compared to the content lifecycle.

Folders have the same lifecycle as content, with the only difference being it has no reference to ContentStore. So, the ContentStore lifecycle is not applicable to folders.

Users and groups have the same lifecycle as folders but they cannot be archived in Alfresco. Once deleted, they are permanently deleted from the system and there is no rollback.

Summary

In this chapter, we covered details about the core components of Alfresco. ContentStore and the database are the building blocks of Alfresco. These two components form your full repository.

Alfresco provides you with various different types of ContentStore, like file storage, an encrypted store, and a caching store. Based on the system design, we can use any of them. Alfresco also provides you with the flexibility to define multiple stores and content can be bound to their own specific stores.

We also discussed the database schemas of Alfresco and a few of the important tables and their associations. Content in any ECM system has a lifecycle. Content moves from live to archive and is then removed from the system. While going through this phase, it impacts all core components.

In the next chapter, we will discuss the important tools and procedures required for the maintenance and troubleshooting of Alfresco.

9 Maintenance and Troubleshooting

Any application, once in production, requires constant monitoring and maintenance to work efficiently. Alfresco as an application can be easily monitored using the JMX interface. This interface is very handy for the system administrator to control and configure applications at run-time without restarting the server. We will learn about JMX configuration and how to use it in detail in this chapter. All applications need some tuning to work as per the requirements. Various components of Alfresco such as the database, thread connection, cache, and logger, need to be configured as per the application.

In this chapter we will look in detail at the following topics:

- Understanding JMX in Alfresco
- Learning about server maintenance and best practices for it
- Understanding audits
- Various ways to tune the Alfresco application

Understanding JMX in Alfresco

JMX knowledge is very important for any system administrator of Alfresco. The JMX technology is a standard part of the JAVA SE platform that provides a simple way to manage applications, devices, and services. Server properties can be edited and the logger can be enabled without restarting the application. There are various open source tools available in the market such as **JConsole**, **VisualVM**, **JMap**, and so on, which allow you to connect to the JMX interface of the application remotely. JConsole is part of the JavaVM, it is an executable file located at `JDK_HOME/bin`.

Refer to `https://docs.oracle.com/javase/tutorial/jmx/overview/index.html` for more details about JMX.

Enabling JMX and connecting to Alfresco through the JMX client

To connect to the Alfresco **MBean** server via the JMX client, you have to do some configuration to turn it on. MBean is a managed Java object and can represent a device, an application, or any resource that needs to be managed. Only the JMX client that supports JSR-160 can connect to the Alfresco MBean server.

Here are the steps to enable JMX in Alfresco:

1. Configure the property below to `true` in the `alfresco-global.properties` file as follows:

   ```
   alfresco.jmx.connector.enabled=true
   ```

2. After starting Alfresco, use a JMX client such as JConsole or VisualVM to connect remotely with Alfresco JMX using the following JMX URL and default credentials:

   ```
   URL:  service:jmx:rmi:///jndi/rmi://<Alfresco_Hostname>:50500/
   alfresco/jmxrmi
   User: controlRole
   Password: change_asap
   ```

The default username and password for the JMX connection should be changed immediately. Make sure you set a strong password:

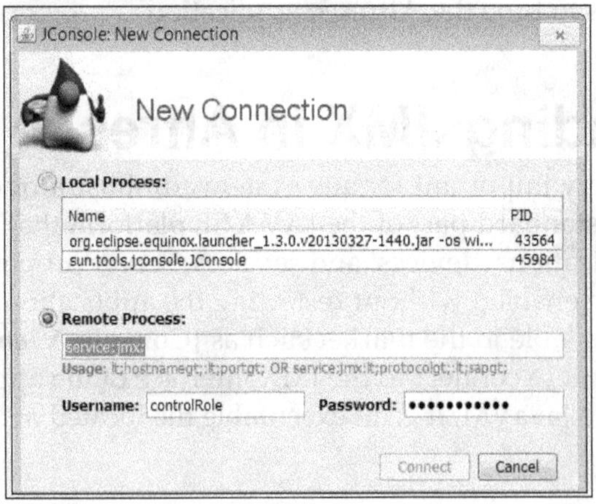
JConsole: New Connection
New Connection
Local Process:
Name
PID
org.eclipse.equinox.launcher_1.3.0.v20130327-1440.jar -os wi...
43564
sun.tools.jconsole.JConsole
45984
Remote Process:
service:jmx:
Username:
controlRole
Password:
Connect
Cancel

The following steps should be followed to change the password and set up proper access for the user:

1. Create a file named `alfresco-jmxrmi.password`. This file will have the user credentials for the JMX connection. Add a username and password as per your organization's policy. Make sure you set a strong password:

   ```
   monitorRole change_asap
   controlRole change_asap
   monitorRole change_asap
   controlRole change_asap
   ```

2. Now a second file is required to be named `alfresco-jmxrmi.access`. This file is required to define the access of the user. There are two kinds of access you can provide: `read-only`, which will allow a user to only monitor the application and `read/write`, which grants access to read and write MBean attributes. The user can execute operations such as enabling the logger, executing the scheduler, and so on.

   ```
   monitorRolereadonly
   controlRolereadwrite
   monitorRole readonly
   controlRole readwrite
   ```

3. Now copy this file to a location where only the application user has access, as the JMX access password is in plain text in the file.
4. Add the `jmx` entry location in the `alfresco-global.properties` file:

   ```
   alfresco.jmx.dir=<Location of JMX files>
   ```

5. You can also configure these values in JVM arguments:

   ```
   -Dcom.sun.management.jmxremote
   -Dcom.sun.management.jmxremote.ssl=false
   -Dcom.sun.management.jmxremote.access.file=<access file path>
   -Dcom.sun.management.jmxremote.password.file=<password file path>
   -Dcom.sun.management.jmxremote.authenticate=true.
   ```

Server administration and monitoring via JMX

Alfresco exposes many MBeans to allow system administrators to monitor and manage the application at runtime. When you connect via a JMX supported client such as JConsole, VisualVM, and so on, the first thing that you will observe is the CPU and memory utilization of the application. It gives you current statistics about the application's performance. The CPU and memory are generally provided by JVM. Refer to the following screenshot:

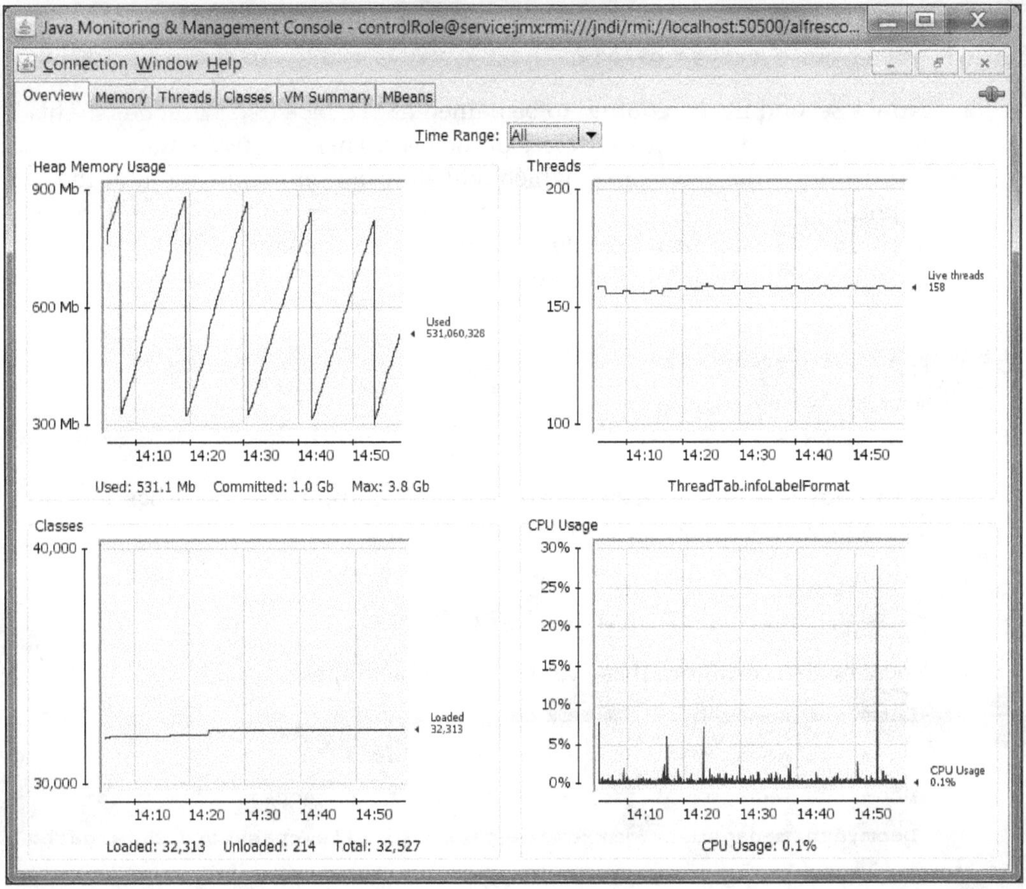
Java Monitoring & Management Console - controlRole@service:jmx:rmi:///jndi/rmi://localhost:50500/alfresco...
Connection Window Help
Overview Memory Threads Classes VM Summary MBeans
Time Range: All
Heap Memory Usage
900 Mb
600 Mb
300 Mb
Used 531,060,328
14:10 14:20 14:30 14:40 14:50
Used: 531.1 Mb Committed: 1.0 Gb Max: 3.8 Gb
Threads
200
150
100
Live threads 158
14:10 14:20 14:30 14:40 14:50
ThreadTab.infoLabelFormat
Classes
40,000
30,000
Loaded 32,313
14:10 14:20 14:30 14:40 14:50
Loaded: 32,313 Unloaded: 214 Total: 32,527
CPU Usage
30%
25%
20%
15%
10%
5%
0%
CPU Usage 0.1%
14:10 14:20 14:30 14:40 14:50
CPU Usage: 0.1%

The **Thread** tab provides you with details about the current thread in execution. You can also investigate each thread. VisualVM also allows you to do sampling which provides you with more details about which thread is taking more CPU time. These tools can also enable thread dumping.

There is a tab named **MBeans** which has the list of all the beans and related operations exposed by Alfresco and JVM. JConsole already provides this MBean feature, if you are using VisualVM you might have to install the MBean plugin. Let's go through the important one required by system administrators.

Each bean has attributes and operations. Attributes are read-only information exposed by these beans. The `Operations` section exposes different actions to manipulate data or trigger some actions. All beans are grouped into a different category

Understanding MBeans and configuration

Alfresco provides details about the server database, content store, user information, schedulers, and so on. All the subsystems such as `FileServerConfig`, `Search`, `Google docs` are also available for configuration via JMX. Refer to the following screenshot.

- `Authority:`

  This provides details about the total number of users and groups in Alfresco. Select the `Attributes` section to view all the details.

- `ConnectionPool:`

  This bean shows details about the database connection. The **Attributes** section will provide details such as active connection, idle connection, initial size of connection, and so on. If you want to see the connection stats in a graph format, click on the value section for any of the fields.

- `Operations`:

  This section allows you fetch more current information. For example the `getUrl` method provides you with database connection information. Similarly, other methods can be executed. This bean is mostly read-only; it will not allow you to change any configuration settings.

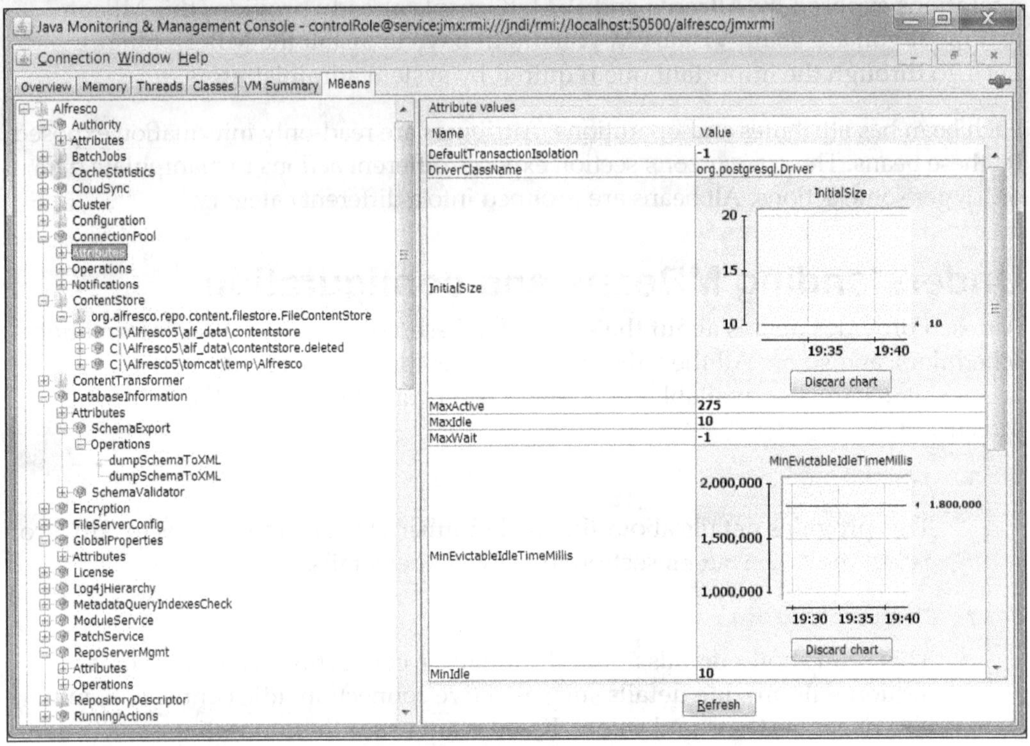
Java Monitoring & Management Console - controlRole@service:jmx:rmi:///jndi/rmi://localhost:50500/alfresco/jmxrmi
Connection Window Help
Overview
Memory
Threads
Classes
VM Summary
MBeans
Alfresco
Authority
Attributes
BatchJobs
CacheStatistics
CloudSync
Cluster
Configuration
ConnectionPool
Attributes
Operations
Notifications
ContentStore
org.alfresco.repo.content.filestore.FileContentStore
C|\Alfresco5\alf_data\contentstore
C|\Alfresco5\alf_data\contentstore.deleted
C|\Alfresco5\tomcat\temp\Alfresco
ContentTransformer
DatabaseInformation
Attributes
SchemaExport
Operations
dumpSchemaToXML
dumpSchemaToXML
SchemaValidator
Encryption
FileServerConfig
GlobalProperties
Attributes
License
Log4jHierarchy
MetadataQueryIndexesCheck
ModuleService
PatchService
RepoServerMgmt
Attributes
Operations
RepositoryDescriptor
RunningActions
Attribute values
Name
Value
DefaultTransactionIsolation
-1
DriverClassName
org.postgresql.Driver
InitialSize
InitialSize
20
15
10
10
19:35
19:40
Discard chart
MaxActive
275
MaxIdle
10
MaxWait
-1
MinEvictableIdleTimeMillis
MinEvictableIdleTimeMillis
2,000,000
1,800,000
1,500,000
1,000,000
19:30
19:35
19:40
Discard chart
MinIdle
10
Refresh

- `ContentStore`:

  This bean shows details about the file storage in Alfresco. The `Attributes` section for each ContentStore will show the space used and the free space available. It also shows the size of the `temp` directory configured for Alfresco. Refer to the following screenshot:

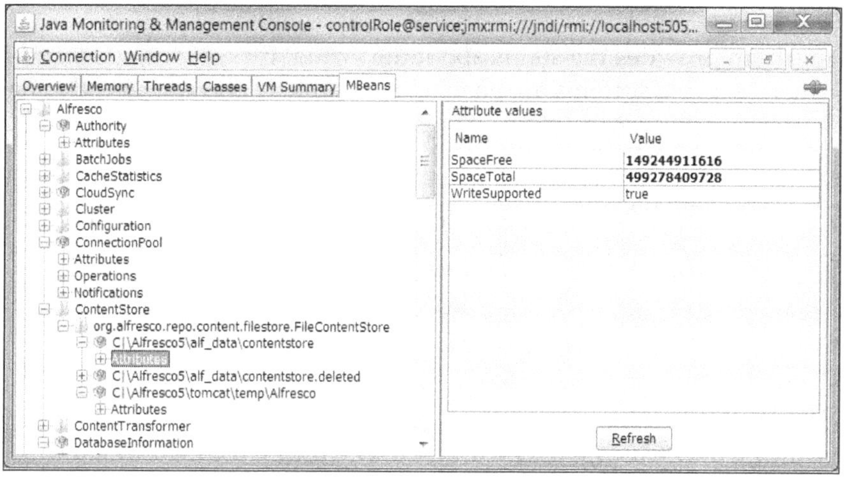

- `DatabaseInformation:`

  This bean provide information related to the database used by the Alfresco application. The `Attributes` section will provide details about the database version, the driver details, and the user connected to the database.

  As per the following screenshot there is one more additional section, the `SchemaExport`. Using the `dumpSchemaToXML` operations, a user can export the complete schema of the database in an `.xml` file.

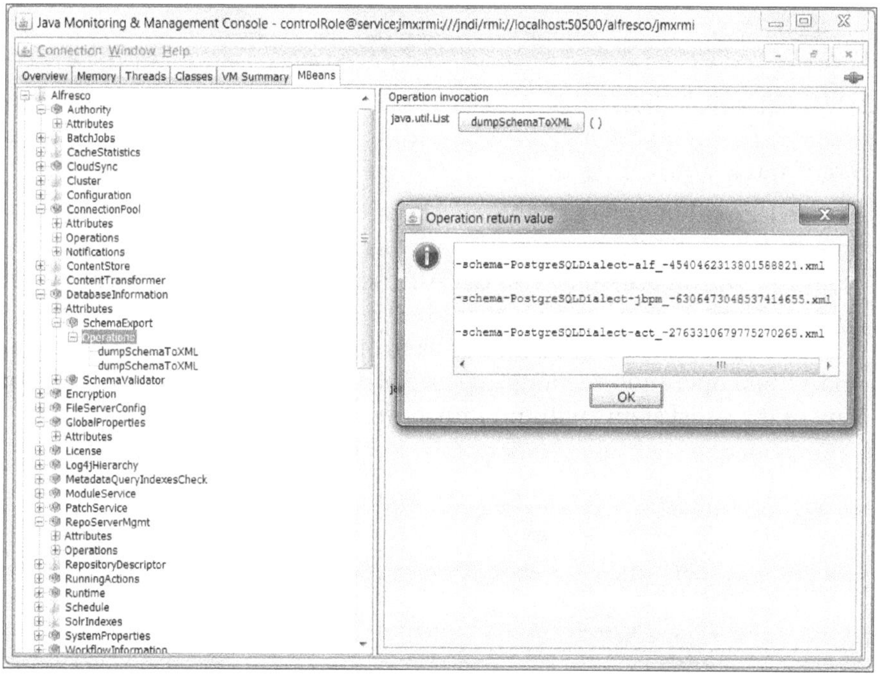

- `FileServerConfig:`

  This bean provides the status about the virtual filesystems, CIFS and FTP. Either these file systems are enabled or disabled. You can directly enable/disable any of the filesystems using the set operations as shown in the following screenshot:

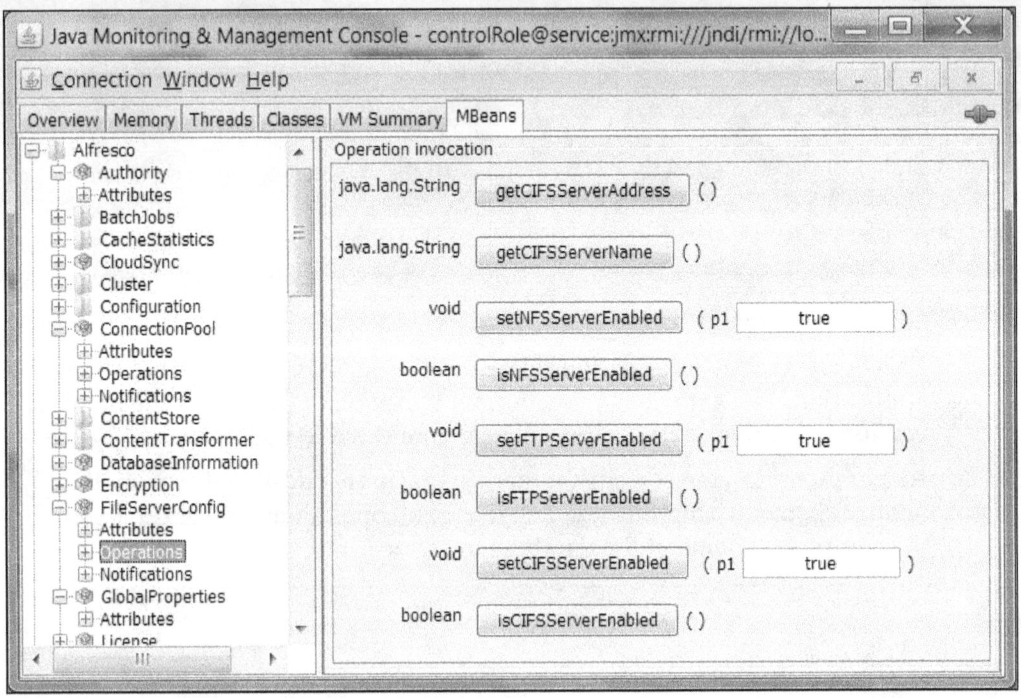

Java Monitoring & Management Console - controlRole@service:jmx:rmi:///jndi/rmi://lo...
Connection Window Help
Overview Memory Threads Classes VM Summary MBeans
Alfresco
Authority
Attributes
BatchJobs
CacheStatistics
CloudSync
Cluster
Configuration
ConnectionPool
Attributes
Operations
Notifications
ContentStore
ContentTransformer
DatabaseInformation
Encryption
FileServerConfig
Attributes
Operations
Notifications
GlobalProperties
Attributes
License
Operation invocation
java.lang.String getCIFSServerAddress ()
java.lang.String getCIFSServerName ()
void setNFSServerEnabled (p1 true)
boolean isNFSServerEnabled ()
void setFTPServerEnabled (p1 true)
boolean isFTPServerEnabled ()
void setCIFSServerEnabled (p1 true)
boolean isCIFSServerEnabled ()

- `Configuration:`

  As we learned in earlier chapters, Alfresco has the concept of a subsystem to separate the important functionality as an individual entity. This `Configuration` bean clubs all the Alfresco subsystem configuration such as `Audit`, `Google docs`, `Email`, `Transformers`, and so on, together. Here you can change the property related to each of the subsystems. Also there are individual operation sections exposed which allow you to start and stop any of the subsystems without impacting the Alfresco server.

- `GlobalProperties:`

  As the name suggests this is a read-only bean which provides details about all the properties in Alfresco.

- `RepoServerMgmt:`

  This bean provides details about user sessions. In Alfresco, for each user session a unique ticket is created. This bean provides a count of active user sessions and active ticket IDs. This is very helpful while grabbing the system statistics for performance tuning. As per the following screenshot, use the `Operations` available or the `Attributes` section to provide all the details.

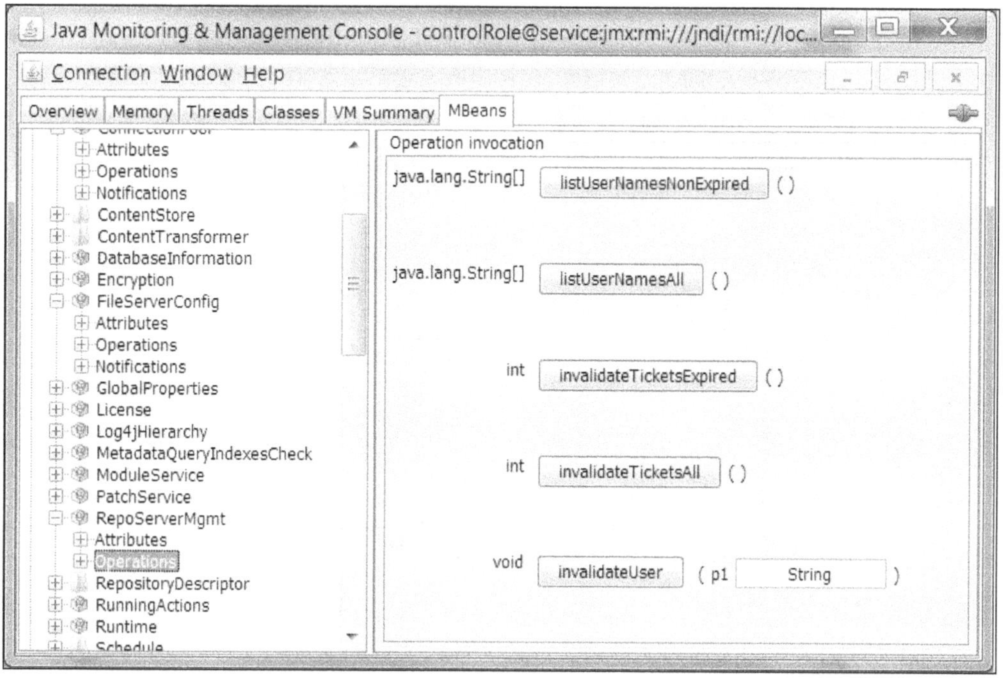
Java Monitoring & Management Console - controlRole@service:jmx:rmi:///jndi/rmi://loc...
Connection Window Help
Overview Memory Threads Classes VM Summary MBeans
Attributes
Operations
Notifications
ContentStore
ContentTransformer
DatabaseInformation
Encryption
FileServerConfig
Attributes
Operations
Notifications
GlobalProperties
License
Log4jHierarchy
MetadataQueryIndexesCheck
ModuleService
PatchService
RepoServerMgmt
Attributes
Operations
RepositoryDescriptor
RunningActions
Runtime
Operation invocation
java.lang.String[] listUserNamesNonExpired ( )
java.lang.String[] listUserNamesAll ( )
int invalidateTicketsExpired ( )
int invalidateTicketsAll ( )
void invalidateUser (p1 String)

- `RepositoryDescriptor:`

  This provides details about the repository version. You can identify the edition and the version of Alfresco. It also provides the version number of the initially installed version. Initially installed and current version details will differ if Alfresco is being upgraded from any older version.

- `Schedule:`

  As the name suggest this bean provides details about all the schedulers available in Alfresco. Schedulers are jobs which are executed at a specified time. You can configure and execute any scheduler runtime in Alfresco. This is a very important bean and so use this cautiously as you can trigger any system schedulers at any point of time. As shown in the following screenshot under `MonitoredCronTrigger` there is a list of scheduled jobs available in Alfresco.

  The `Attributes` section will show when the job is scheduled to be executed, when it was executed, and other details. Operations have a bunch of `get` methods and `execute` methods exposed. The `get` methods provide the same details shown in the `Attributes` section. Using the `execute` method you can trigger the job. The job will perform the same operation as it does normally.

  The **Attribute values** tab can be seen by selecting `Attributes`:

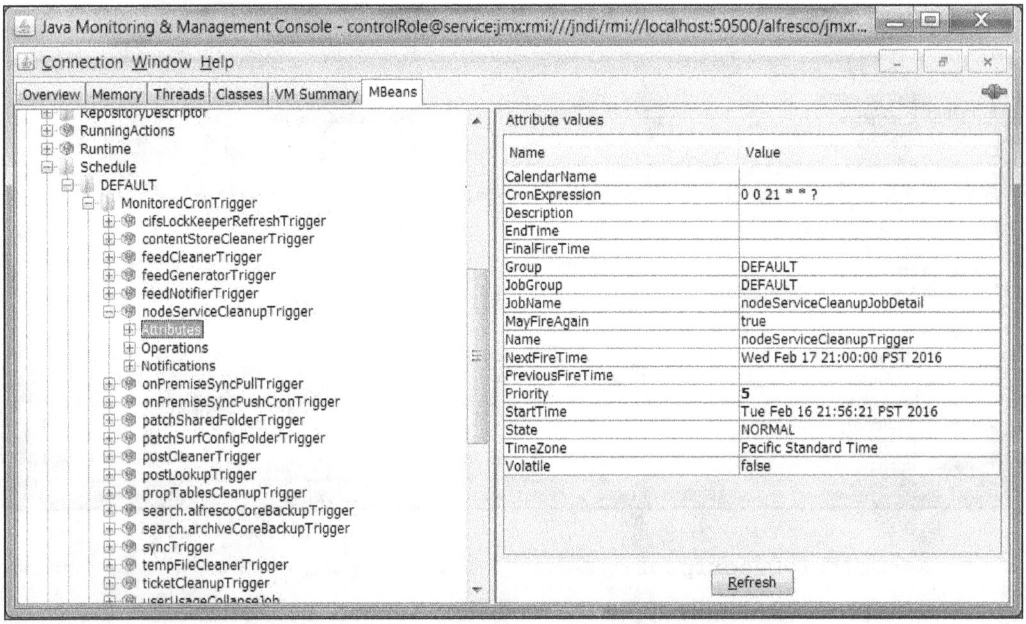
Java Monitoring & Management Console - controlRole@service:jmx:rmi:///jndi/rmi://localhost:50500/alfresco/jmxr...
Connection Window Help
Overview
Memory
Threads
Classes
VM Summary
MBeans
RunningActions
Runtime
Schedule
DEFAULT
MonitoredCronTrigger
cifsLockKeeperRefreshTrigger
contentStoreCleanerTrigger
feedCleanerTrigger
feedGeneratorTrigger
feedNotifierTrigger
nodeServiceCleanupTrigger
Attributes
Operations
Notifications
onPremiseSyncPullTrigger
onPremiseSyncPushCronTrigger
patchSharedFolderTrigger
patchSurfConfigFolderTrigger
postCleanerTrigger
postLookupTrigger
propTablesCleanupTrigger
search.alfrescoCoreBackupTrigger
search.archiveCoreBackupTrigger
syncTrigger
tempFileCleanerTrigger
ticketCleanupTrigger
Attribute values
Name
Value
CalendarName
CronExpression
0 0 21 * * ?
Description
EndTime
FinalFireTime
Group
DEFAULT
JobGroup
DEFAULT
JobName
nodeServiceCleanupJobDetail
MayFireAgain
true
Name
nodeServiceCleanupTrigger
NextFireTime
Wed Feb 17 21:00:00 PST 2016
PreviousFireTime
Priority
5
StartTime
Tue Feb 16 21:56:21 PST 2016
State
NORMAL
TimeZone
Pacific Standard Time
Volatile
false
Refresh

On selecting `Operations`, we see the **Operation invocation** tab:

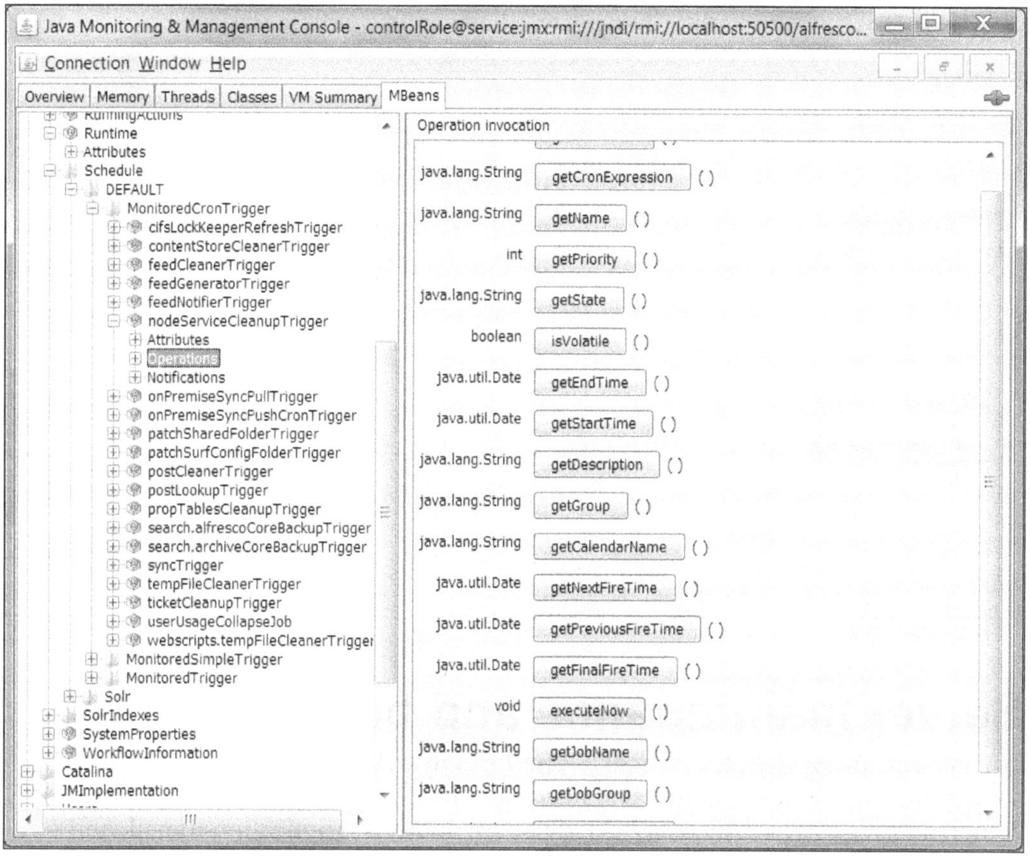
Java Monitoring & Management Console - controlRole@service:jmx:rmi:///jndi/rmi://localhost:50500/alfresco...
Connection Window Help
Overview
Memory
Threads
Classes
VM Summary
MBeans
Runtime
Attributes
Schedule
DEFAULT
MonitoredCronTrigger
cifsLockKeeperRefreshTrigger
contentStoreCleanerTrigger
feedCleanerTrigger
feedGeneratorTrigger
feedNotifierTrigger
nodeServiceCleanupTrigger
Attributes
Operations
Notifications
onPremiseSyncPullTrigger
onPremiseSyncPushCronTrigger
patchSharedFolderTrigger
patchSurfConfigFolderTrigger
postCleanerTrigger
postLookupTrigger
propTablesCleanupTrigger
search.alfrescoCoreBackupTrigger
search.archiveCoreBackupTrigger
syncTrigger
tempFileCleanerTrigger
ticketCleanupTrigger
userUsageCollapseJob
webscripts.tempFileCleanerTrigger
MonitoredSimpleTrigger
MonitoredTrigger
Solr
SolrIndexes
SystemProperties
WorkflowInformation
Catalina
JMImplementation
Operation invocation
java.lang.String getCronExpression ( )
java.lang.String getName ( )
int getPriority ( )
java.lang.String getState ( )
boolean isVolatile ( )
java.util.Date getEndTime ( )
java.util.Date getStartTime ( )
java.lang.String getDescription ( )
java.lang.String getGroup ( )
java.lang.String getCalendarName ( )
java.util.Date getNextFireTime ( )
java.util.Date getPreviousFireTime ( )
java.util.Date getFinalFireTime ( )
void executeNow ( )
java.lang.String getJobName ( )
java.lang.String getJobGroup ( )

- `Log4j`:

  As the name suggests, this bean allows you to set a different log level for any available class. This is very helpful while debugging. You can turn on the logger for any class runtime in the production system and monitor the logs. Once analysis is completed you can turn off the log or set it to a minimum level.

As shown in the following screenshot, select `Attributes` and on the right-hand side, edit the priority for the selected class. The priority can be `INFO`, `DEBUG`, or `WARN`. Changes will have an immediate impact.

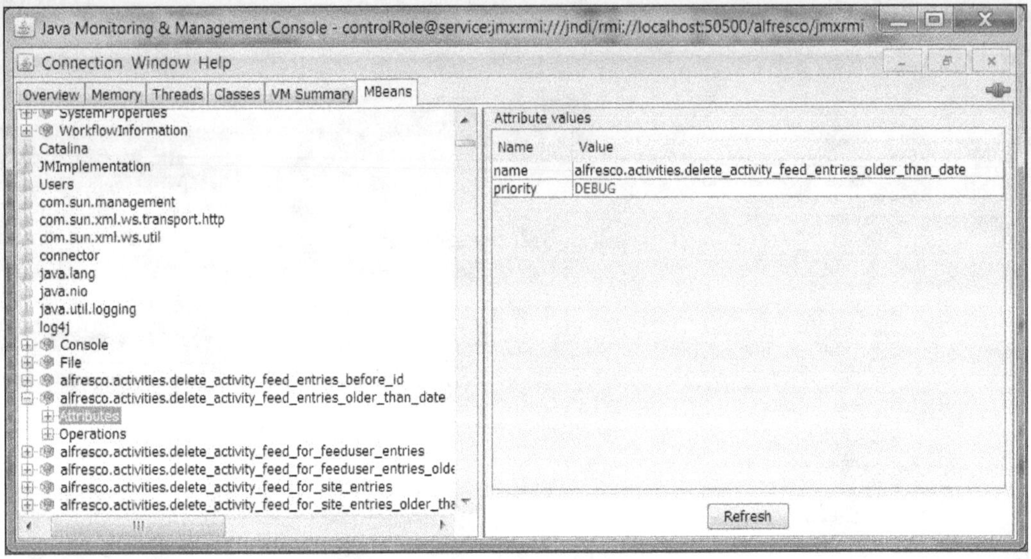
Java Monitoring & Management Console - controlRole@service:jmx:rmi:///jndi/rmi://localhost:50500/alfresco/jmxrmi
Connection Window Help
Overview
Memory
Threads
Classes
VM Summary
MBeans
WorkflowInformation
Catalina
JMImplementation
Users
com.sun.management
com.sun.xml.ws.transport.http
com.sun.xml.ws.util
connector
java.lang
java.nio
java.util.logging
log4j
Console
File
alfresco.activities.delete_activity_feed_entries_before_id
alfresco.activities.delete_activity_feed_entries_older_than_date
Attributes
Operations
alfresco.activities.delete_activity_feed_for_feeduser_entries
alfresco.activities.delete_activity_feed_for_site_entries
Attribute values
Name
Value
name
alfresco.activities.delete_activity_feed_entries_older_than_date
priority
DEBUG
Refresh

Server maintenance and best practices

To maintain any system and to make it perform in an optimal manner requires some tuning as per the organization needs and load on the application. Different components of Alfresco such as JVM, database, indexes, application thread, and so on, need to be tuned as per the system needs. Default settings work with less data sets.

Let's look at the different aspects of server maintenance and tuning.

Understanding JVM settings

Java memory and garbage collections settings are mainly associated with repository usage. Based on the number of concurrent users using the system, the amount of read/write operations will help you to decide the memory settings. As per Alfresco it is recommended to use a 64 bit machine and JVM. A 32 bit machine will not provide optimal performance. Also make sure the clock speed is above 2.5 Gz.

A few important tips while tuning JVM include:

- Make sure the following settings are being set in JVM:
  `XX:+UseConcMarkSweepGC -XX:+CMSIncrementalMode -server`
- Based on your usage properly set the `X` ms and `X` mx size. Make sure `XX:MaxPermSize` is at least more than 128 MB.
- Make sure you reserve enough memory for OS and other operations. Also `X` mx should not exceed the available RAM.
- For a normal production system, it is recommended to have 8 GB RAM for Alfresco. Alfresco stores a lot of cache data in memory, so enough memory allocation is required to have optimal performance.
- After tuning, validate the memory usage using JConsole and set parameters as per the observation. Refer to the standard Java documentation to tune JVM.

Maintenance of disk space

Alfresco stores the binary file in a file system. So calculation of disk space is easy. Calculate the average file size and the number of files your repository will have and based on that you can decide the disk space to be used. Keep room for temporary operations. If your application needs versioning, make sure you keep room for that. Every version copy will create new content in the filesystem. So technically it will double the size of disk space required.

From a hardware perspective, Alfresco does not have any specific recommendations, but it is better to use a fast disk so the read/write operation will be faster. Always monitor the I/O performance for the disk to make sure there is no bottleneck. Quite often the time of disk I/O is the main reason for slow server performance. Threads will be stuck waiting to read/write files.

From a maintenance perspective, the points below are the items a system admin needs to take care with:

- Regularly monitor the I/O performance of the disk.
- Setup monitoring tools in your organization which can monitor the I/O performance and network performance.
- Make sure the temporary files unused in the system are cleaned.

- Ensure that old log files are being archived and moved to other low end disks.
- Make sure content is being removed from the trash can as per the defined policy. This will allow the orphan cleaner process to clean-up the data from `contentstore`.
- Make sure that files in `contentstore.deleted` are being cleaned at regular intervals which will give room for `contentstore`.
- Have a strong backup plan for copying `contentstore`. Make sure this copy process does not overload your NAS and OS system.
- If you are using **Lucene** make sure the indexes are on a local disk. Carry out regular full indexing/partial indexing based in some defined intervals on index size. This will help to keep the data clean.

DB monitoring and tuning

The monitoring database is very critical for Alfresco applications. System administrators need to make sure there is no deadlock and threads are not getting stuck. Database performance plays an important role in overall application performance.

From a maintenance and tuning perspective, system administrators need to take care of the following aspects:

- Setup a standard DB monitoring tool based on the database used. Oracle comes with its own monitoring tool. For MySQL you can use `innodb` to get the stats.
- Tools should allow you to monitor the number of open connections, queries being executing, provide statistics about the number of insert/update queries, and it should also provide details about where the connections are being opened.
- Use this tool regularly to monitor the database connections. If there are stale connections try to troubleshoot the reason for that.
- Make sure the allowed DB connections are set as per system usage in Alfresco. Let's assume the Alfresco `db` connection pool size is `40`, then the allowed `db` connection pool in the database should be higher. If you have a clustered environment it will be double the value.
- The Alfresco `db.pool.max` should not be greater than the database connection pool size. The application thread size should also be inline with the allowed database connection. For example, in the Tomcat `server.xml` file, `conf` has a configuration related to `maxThreads`. Configure this value appropriately.

- Refer to `http://tomcat.apache.org/tomcat-7.0-doc/config/executor.html`.
- The DB should be provided with enough RAM and disk space. For the normal standard Alfresco application provide around 4 GB of RAM to the DB server.
- Also set up a tool which can monitor CPU and memory usage of the database.
- The DB server should be on a separate machine from Alfresco.

Schedulers

Schedulers are background jobs which execute based on the specified schedule. In Alfresco there are various application jobs and system cleanup jobs. Here we will understand the list of scheduled jobs available and depending on the system needs these schedulers can be turned on or off. Some schedulers have a CPU intensive-operation which should always be executed at night when the system load is less.

Let's go through the important schedulers which are important for a system administrator. A list of all the schedulers is also available via JMX which we covered in previous sections about Alfresco:

- Content store cleaner:

  This scheduler is to clean up the content store and move the orphan content (that is, the binary files which are not refereed by any node in Alfresco) from the `contentstore` to the `contenstore.deleted` directory. This scheduler should always be executed when the system load is less. Once the content is moved to the `contentstore.deleted` folder, the system admin can manually remove the file from this directory.

  Configure the following properties in `alfresco-global.properties` to execute this scheduler. You can also manually trigger this scheduler using JMX:

  ```
  system.content.orphanProtectDays=14<Define how long the orphan
  should be kept before it can be deleted>

  system.content.orphanCleanup.cronExpression=0 0 4   ? <Cron
  expression define the time of execution.Default is every 4>
  ```

- Node Service Cleanup:

  This scheduler is responsible for cleaning-up the `db` entry of permanently deleted nodes. Once any node is permanently deleted from Alfresco, there are a few entries still present in the database as we learned in the previous chapter, *Chapter 8, The Basics of the Alfresco Content Store*. By default this is configured to execute daily at 9 P.M. You can change the timings by configuring the `cron` expression in the bean `nodeServiceCleanupTrigger` via JMX.

- Temp File Cleaner:

  This scheduler cleans the temporary file created in the application `temp` directory. By default the scheduler executes every 30 minutes. There is no need to change these values. You can change the timings via JMX.

Fetching audit records from Alfresco

In Alfresco all the actions performed by any user are audited and stored in the Alfresco database. These records can be fetched any time by the admin user. There is web-script exposed which can be used to fetch and delete the audit entries from Alfresco. This can be only performed by admin users. We learned about audit configuration in *Chapter 3, Alfresco Configuration*.

To fetch the audit records from Alfresco there is a `get` service exposed by Alfresco, which can be found at the following URL.

- `/alfresco/service/api/audit/query/{application}?fromId={fromId}&toId={toId}&fromTime={fromTime}&toTime={toTime}&user={user}&forward={forward}&limit={limit}&verbose={verbose}`

The parameters involved are explained as follows:

- `application`: Audits are divided into different applications. By default everything is under `alfresco-access`. So pass the application name as `alfresco-access`.
- `fromId&toId`: If you know the audit ID number you can use these parameters. Mostly you can skip them.
- `fromTime&toTime`: This passes the time in milliseconds to fetch the audit record based on a specified duration.
- `user`: This parameter will allow you to fetch audit records for a specified user.
- `limit`: This parameter will limit the number of audit records in response. Make sure you use this parameter so that the system is not overloaded and fetches a lot of audit records.

- `verbose`: This parameter can be false/true. If true it will send more details in the JSON response.

Alfresco also allows you to delete audit records. You can call the following POST URL to delete the records, pass the application name, and duration of time for which audit records need to be deleted:

- `/alfresco/service/api/audit/clear/{application}?fromTime={fromTime}&toTime={toTime}`

Use this service cautiously, as it will remove the audit records permanently from the system. Also try to provide a small duration so that the system doesn't get overloaded.

Tips for troubleshooting the application

The system admin should know a few Alfresco troubleshooting techniques. Let's go through the common errors we see in Alfresco applications and the required debug points:

- **Alfresco system in read-only mode**: The main reason for this exception is license expiration. Make sure the license is valid and if required, update the new license. If you have to restore the system from any backup and you see this error make sure the license file is not corrupted.
- **Context initialization failure**: This error can happen when the database and `contentstore` are not in sync. It is very important to have both of these components in sync for Alfresco to work properly. Another reason for these errors could be the permission on `contentstore`. The Alfresco application user should have full access to `contentstore`.
- **Degraded system performance**: For troubleshooting this case, monitor the CPU and memory usage of Alfresco. Also monitor the I/O performance and database connection. This will help to isolate the cause of the slowness. Try to a take few thread dumps to see more details about what operation is currently being performed and where the threads are stuck.

Summary

In this chapter we covered details about JMX in Alfresco. An admin can monitor the application and also configure Alfresco via JMX. There are different beans such as Schedule, Database, Connection Pool, Logger, and so on which can be configured without a system restart. We also covered important aspects from the server maintenance perspective. There are monitoring tools required by the system admin to control the database, disk, and applications.

This chapter also provided details about how an admin can easily fetch the audit records from the system. This will also help to analyze whether unauthorized activity has been performed.

In the next chapter we will discuss the upgrade process of Alfresco. We will go through the step-by-step process to upgrade from one version of Alfresco to any other version of Alfresco.

10
Upgrade

Alfresco releases new versions for new features, enhancements, and improvements to the system. From time to time, it is necessary to upgrade to the latest version of Alfresco. Upgrading is a process that involves moving all the data stored in the X version of Alfresco to an updated Y version of Alfresco. It is always recommended to move to the latest release; there are different paths for upgrading, which we will cover in detail in this chapter.

We will cover the following topics in this chapter:

- The importance of choosing the correct path for the upgrade
- Understanding the upgrade process
- Troubleshooting and best practices for upgrading Alfresco

Understanding the Alfresco upgrade process

Upgrading Alfresco is a multi-step process. Based on how customizations are done and what new features available, you will need to first decide the target version of Alfresco. Based on the currently installed version, there could be different paths to upgrade it.

Upgrading involves moving all the content (database, content store, indexes) to a new version of Alfresco, and any feature customization done in Alfresco needs to be upgraded to make it compatible with the new system. The last step is to validate the whole system and data.

Now let's go through each of the steps in detail.

Choosing the upgrade path

Alfresco's major versions are 2.x, 3.x, 4.x, and 5.x. 2.x is the oldest version and 5.0 is the latest version available in Alfresco. Recently, Alfresco has stopped support for any version older than 4.x.

The standard upgrade process is if your current Alfresco system version is 2.x, then you cannot directly upgrade to 4.x or 5.0 as there are major functionality changes. Alfresco recommends you go to an intermediate stable version before upgrading to the final version.

Here are a few samples of upgrading Alfresco Enterprise versions:

- **Current version is 2.x and target version is 5.0**: Since you cannot directly upgrade Alfresco to v5.0, you will first need to upgrade to a stable version of Alfresco 3.x, then to 4.x, and finally you can upgrade to 5.0.

  2.x -> 3.x-> 4.x -> 5.0

- **Current version is 3.x and target version is 5.0**: Again, here you need to upgrade to 4.x first before you can upgrade to 5.0 as there are major database changes. For example, there are index changes in version 5.0.

Before deciding on an upgrade path, it is very important to contact Alfresco Support to get information about the complete upgrade path.

Also, before you choose the target version for the upgrade, there are a few important points that need to be considered:

- Get a proper understanding of the new features and changes available in the latest version of Alfresco. For example, Alfresco Explorer is deprecated in v5.0, so if your end users are using Explorer, then you might only want to upgrade to the latest stable 4.x version.
- Conduct an analysis of the effect of any customization done to the current version of Alfresco.
- Decide your timeline for the upgrade process.

Standard upgrade guidelines

All upgrades have standard guidelines that need to be followed regardless of the version you are upgrading to. Let's go through each of the steps in detail.

Preparing a checklist

Analyzing the current system and the new, target upgraded system is very important for the upgrade and for proper planning. The first step should be getting details about the current infrastructure: type of environment, the amount of customization done, important features used, data size, and so on.

The second step is to decide on the target upgrade version and understand all the features that your current application will have and decide if there is an alternative. Once the target version of Alfresco is selected, identify all software requirements and environment details from Alfresco Support. For example, when you are upgrading to the latest version of Alfresco, you might have to change the JDK version, application server version, and other things. The system stack might also require changes: the Solr version might need to be upgraded.

Prepare a checklist of the new system requirements and validation process.

Setup and validation of the new environment

Install the new Alfresco version on a separate server from the production system. Refer to *Chapter 2, Setting Up the Alfresco Environment*, for the installation process. Validate installation has been done correctly and has been documented.

If you have a distributed clustered environment, enable clustering and validate the application is working as expected. Don't use production data yet, validate with a blank database and content store first. For an Alfresco 5 clustering setup, refer to *Chapter 7, High Availability in Alfresco.*

If your current Alfresco application has code customization or extensions deployed, make sure all code is made compatible with the new version. Also, make sure all configuration changes done on the old server are also configured properly on the new Alfresco server.

Deploy all the customized code and configuration on the new Alfresco server and perform a regression test. Make sure your existing application works properly with the new version of Alfresco. All this validation is very important prior to upgrading.

Data upgrade process

Once you have validated that the new Alfresco server has been installed and configured properly, it is time to actually upgrade the data. The following steps need to be performed:

1. Take a backup of data from `Production`, which will be used for upgrade purposes. You need to take a backup from the `Database`, `ContentStore` repository, and indexes. This will be your snapshot of data which will be upgraded to the latest version of Alfresco. Refer to the following properties in their respective files to locate the data to be backed up:

   ```
   dir.root=<Content store location. Property configured in alfresco-global.properties>
   db.url =<Database connection details. Property configured in alfresco-global.properties>
   data.dir.root=<Solr Index location. Propertyconfigured in solrcore.properties for both workspace and archive indexes>
   dir.indexes=<Lucene index path. Property configured in alfresco-global.properties>
   ```

2. Restore the database `ContentStore` and indexes on a separate server. If we keep the upgraded environment separate, then the production server can still be used and will not be impacted.
3. As discussed in the installation and validation sections, once the new version of the Alfresco server has been completely tested with customized code and configurations, make sure the server has stopped.
4. Configure the following properties in the `alfresco-global.properties` file to point to the restored production database and content store in step 2. For details about database and content store configuration you can refer to *Chapter 3, Alfresco Configuration*, and *Chapter 8, The Basics of the Alfresco Content Store*. Make sure all your test data is wiped out in the new installation:

   ```
   dir.root=<Restored content store location>
   db.username=<Set correct alfresco database username>
   db.password=<Alfresco database password>
   db.name=<Database name>
   db.url=<Full Database URL>
   ```

5. Point Solr indexes to the new restored indexes. Remove all the test data and model files created in the new installation. Configure the following properties for the Solr indexes in the `alfresco-global.properties` file. Also make sure all the old Solr configuration are also copied to a new instance:

   ```
   index.subsystem.name= <Set proper subsystem name>
   ```

6. Configure the following property in `solrcore.properties` to point to new indexes for both the workspace and archive:

```
data.dir.root=<Set the full path for the indexes>
```

7. If you are upgrading to Alfresco 5.0, there are a few additional steps required to upgrade the Solr version, as Alfresco v5.0 uses Solr4. We will cover these details later in the chapter.
8. If you are upgrading from Alfresco prior to version 4.x make sure the following jbpm properties are set to `true` to enable the `jbpm` engine, because in the latest version of Alfresco the workflow engine has been changed to activity, and by default activity is enabled:

```
system.workflow.engine.jbpm.enabled=true
```

9. Start the Alfresco server and monitor the logs. Log files will provide you with details about the upgrade process. If you have a clustered environment, you can configure all nodes with the same code and configurations. Start only one node. Later on you can restart all the other nodes and all of them will have upgraded data.
10. Once the upgrade is finished and the server starts properly, validate the upgraded server.
11. If the server is validated properly and all goes well, you can switch over to the new upgraded server and the old production server can be shut down. If there is an issue with the new upgraded server, the old production server can always be turned back on.

Solr upgrade process for Alfresco 5

Alfresco 5.x only supports Solr4. It doesn't support Lucene or older versions of Solr any more. To completely upgrade to Alfresco 5, the system has to recalculate all the indexes with the latest version. If the current system is using Lucene indexes, then the system needs to be upgraded to Solr before we can upgrade to Solr4.

Let's go through the steps to upgrade Solr:

1. If the current repository is using Lucene indexes and is an older version prior to Alfresco 4.x or on Alfresco 4.x, then you need to upgrade the system to Alfresco 4.x. Set up a new Solr1 and configure Solr1 tracking to re-calcuate all the indexes. For larger repositories this can be a long process.
2. Once your indexes are using Solr in Alfresco 4.x., the system is ready to upgrade to Alfresco 5.
3. While you are upgrading Alfresco 4.x to Alfresco 5.0, you can still use the old Solr and configure Solr4 to start tracking and recalculating the indexes.

4. During the upgrade process, copy all the Solr indexes from Alfresco 4 to the new installation of Alfresco 5, as we discussed in the upgrade process. Also make sure Alfresco 5 is running properly with the older version of Solr.
5. Once the upgrade is finished, set up the new Solr4 instance on a separate server. It is not recommended to have both Solr and Solr4 on the same machine as the indexing process will be heavy on memory and CPU utilization. Refer to *Chapter 5, Search,* for Solr4 installation details.
6. Verify in the Alfresco admin console that the search subsystem is still set to the older version of Solr.
7. Now configure `solrcore.properties` located in `workspace-SpacesStore/conf` and `archive-SpacesStore/conf` in the new Solr4 installation to point to the new Alfresco server and start tracking the indexes:

```
data.dir.root=<Index Directory location>
enable.alfresco.tracking=<Set to true to start the tracking>
alfresco.host=<Alfresco Server Host>
alfresco.port=<Alfresco Server Port>
alfresco.port.ssl=<Alfresco Server SSL Port>
alfresco.cron=<Cron expression to tracking Alfresco index>
```

8. You can monitor the indexing status of Solr4 using the JMX or by using the following monitor service of Solr:

```
http://<Solr Server Host and Port>/solr4/admin/
cores?action=SUMMARY&wt=xml
```

9. Once Solr4 has indexed the complete repository, verify the report summary count matches the node count in the repository. Switch the search subsystem from Solr to Solr4 using Alfresco admin console or by configuring the following property in the `alfresco-global.properties` file. Stop the older Solr version:

```
index.subsystem.name=solr4
dir.keystore=<New solr certificate location>
solr.port.ssl=<Solr SSL port>
```

[Refer to *Chapter 5, Search,* for details about troubleshooting and accessing Solr Indexes.]

Best practices and troubleshooting

Upgrading Alfresco can be a long process, depending on the repository size. Here are a few tips for administrators that will be helpful in the upgrade process:

- It is recommended to do a dry run of the upgrade process before starting the upgrade process on production data.
- Set up proper monitoring for database server logs and the Alfresco server. Alfresco log monitoring will help troubleshoot any issue faced while upgrading. Database logs will help to troubleshoot if there is any problem with upgrading the database.
- During the upgrade process Alfresco moves the data from the old schema to the new database schema, which can take time depending on the size of the repository.
- Proper regression of customized code with the new version of Alfresco server is required.
- Monitor Solr indexes and do proper data verification.
- From a validation standpoint after upgrade, validate that you are able to search all the existing content, users, and groups. Check that permissions on folders are correct.
- Once the server has been upgraded, based on the performance of the server, check if any tuning is required, for example, JVM settings, index tuning, and so on.

Summary

In this chapter, we covered details about the process of upgrading Alfresco. The Alfresco upgrade process is pretty straightforward; it is just matter of configuring the system. The first step of the upgrade will analyze the system and decide the final path of upgrade. Once the path is decided, set up the new server and validate and start the upgrade process with production data. Make sure Solr indexes are recalculated properly with the new Solr4 version in Alfresco 5.

Index

A

R

S

T

www.ingramcontent.com/pod-product-compliance
Lightning Source LLC
Chambersburg PA
CBHW060132060326
40690CB00018B/3847
9781782175032